Copyright © 2023, Hootsie Hill Educational Programs and Consulting LLC. ALL RIGHTS RESERVED.

No permission is granted to you to copy, reproduce, distribute, transmit, upload, store, display in public, alter, or modify the content herein. You agree not to change or delete any proprietary notices from printed or downloaded materials.

ISBN: 979-8-9885145-0-3

Contents

Unit 1- Scientific Foundations of Psychology (10-14% AP Exam Weighting) 4
    1.1 What is psychology? 4
    1.2 What are the methods psychologist use to study the mind and behavior? 5
    1.3 What is the experimental method, and how does it work? 6
    1.4 What are the strengths and weaknesses of the research methods? 7
    1.5 What statistical techniques do psychological researchers use? 8
    1.6 What are the ethical guidelines researchers must follow when conducting research? 9

Unit 2- Biological Bases of Behavior (8-10% AP Exam Weighting) 11
    2.1 How do heredity, environment, and evolution interact to shape behavior? 11
    2.2 How does the endocrine system affect behavior? 11
    2.3 What are the classifications of the nervous system? 12
    2.4 What is a neuron, its parts, and what are their functions? 13
    2.5 How do drugs influence neural firing? 15
    2.6 What are the brain's structures and their corresponding functions? 15
    2.7 What tools do scientists use for examining the brain? 18
    2.8 How does the brain adapt to its environment? 18
    2.9 What is consciousness? 19

Unit 3- Sensation and Perception (6-8% AP Exam Weighting) 21
    3.1 What are the principles of sensation? 21
    3.2 How does our mind organize and interpret sensory information? 22
    3.3 What are the structures and functions of the parts of the eye? 25
    3.4 How does the mind perceive visual input, and how do those perceptions create illusions? 26
    3.5 What are the structures and functions of the parts of the ear? 28
    3.6 How does the sensory system create smell and taste from chemicals? 29
    3.7 How does the body sense and perceive the world? 29

Unit 4- Learning (7-9% AP Exam Weighting) 31
    4.1 What is learning? 31
    4.2 What is classical conditioning, and how does it work? 31
    4.3 What is operant conditioning, and how does it work? 33
    4.4 What is observational and latent learning, and how do they work? 34
    4.5 How do societal and cognitive factors affect learning? 35

Unit 5- Cognitive Psychology (13-17 % AP Exam Weighting) 37
    5.1 What are the cognitive processes of memory? 37
    5.2 What is encoding, and how does it work? 39
    5.3 What are the principles for the effective storage of memories? 39
    5.4 What are the principles of retrieval of memories? 40
    5.5 What are memory errors, and why are they committed? 41
    5.6 What are the biological bases of memory? 42
    5.7 What are the methods to solve problems? 42
    5.8 What are the obstacles to problem-solving? 43
    5.9 What is intelligence? 44

    5.11 How have psychologists measured intelligence throughout its history? 45

    5.12 How is language produced? 47

Unit 6- Developmental Psychology (7-9% AP Exam Weighting) 49

    6.1 What are the factors of prenatal and childhood physical development? 49

    6.2 What are the social factors of development? 50

    6.3 How do cognitive abilities change throughout life? 51

    6.4 What is adolescence, and what distinguishes it as a unique stage of development? 53

    6.5 What are the cognitive and physical changes of adulthood? 54

    6.6 What are the models of moral development? 55

    6.7 How do gender and sex influence socialization and development? 55

Unit 7- Motivation, Emotion, and Personality (11-15% AP Exam Weighting) 57

    7.1 What are the theories of motivation? 57

    7.2 What are the biological motivators to eat? 58

    7.3 What are the theories of emotions? 60

    7.4 What is stress, and how does it manifest? 62

    7.5 What is personality? 62

    7.6 What is Sigmund Freud's psychoanalytic theory, and how does it differ from other theories? 63

    7.7 What are the social-cognitive theories of personality? 65

    7.8 What is the humanistic perspective of personality? 66

    7.9 What are the similarities and differences of the trait theories? 67

    7.10 How are traits measured? 67

Unit 8- Clinical Psychology (12-16% AP Exam Weighting) 69

    8.1 How do psychologists and psychiatrists diagnose mental illnesses? 69

    8.2 What are the strengths and limitations of explaining psychological disorders? 69

    8.3 What are the major neurodevelopmental and schizophrenic spectrum disorders? What are their symptoms? 70

    8.4 What are the major anxiety and depressive disorders? What are their symptoms? 71

    8.5 What are the major somatic and dissociative disorders? What are their symptoms? 71

    8.6 What are the major eating, substance, addictive, and personality disorders? What are their symptoms? 72

    8.7 What are the major treatment orientations for mental illness, and who is responsible for their development? 73

    8.8 What treatment options for mental illness use a biological approach? 75

Unit 9- Social Psychology (8-10% AP Exam Weighting) 77

    9.1 How do people attribute behavior, and how does it impact one's perception of the world? 77

    9.2 How are attitudes formed and changed? 77

    9.3 How do the situational influences of conformity, compliance, and obedience influence behavior? 78

    9.4 How does the presence of others affect individual behavior? 80

    9.5 What factors contribute to bias, prejudice, and discrimination? 81

    9.6 What is altruism? 81

    9.7 What factors contribute to attraction and love? 81

Unit 1- Scientific Foundations of Psychology (10-14% AP Exam Weighting)

1.1 What is psychology?

Psychology	The scientific study of the mind and behavior.
Behavior	Anything an organism does.

What was psychology before the widespread use of scientific methods?

Monism	Aristotle, John Locke	The mind and body are the same entity.
Dualism	Socrates, Plato, Descartes	The position that the mind and the body constitute two separate realms or substances.
Structuralism	Wilhelm Wundt, Edward Titchener	The study of mental experience. Seeks to investigate the structure of such experience through a systematic program of experiments based on trained introspection.
Functionalism	William James	It emphasizes the causes and consequences of human behavior.
Introspection		The process of attempting to directly access one's own internal psychological processes, judgments, perceptions, or states.

Study Tip- **Key Word System:** Turn names into a visual to remember them better. Ex. Lebron James likes to make funky dunks. William James is a functionalist.

When did psychology become a science?

Empiricism	- The belief in experimentation is the most important, if not the only, foundation of scientific knowledge and how individuals evaluate truth claims or the adequacy of theories and models. - Some approaches to psychology hold that sensory experience is the origin of all knowledge.
Wilhelm Wundt	- Wundt established his psychology laboratory at the University at Leipzig in 1879. - Conducted experiments in reaction time to sensory experiences. - Push a button, and an apparatus would record the time to react.

What are the contemporary psychological approaches, and who are the key contributors?

Perspective	Contributors	Subject Matter	Basic Premise
Behavioral	John B. Watson, Ivan Pavlov, B.F. Skinner	Learning	Only observable events can be studied.
Gestalt	Max Wertheimer	Perception	Visual perceptions are organized by the mind as a whole.
Psychoanalytic	Sigmund Freud, Carl Jung, Alfred Adler	Unconscious Thoughts	Unconscious motives and experiences in early childhood shape personality.
Humanistic	Carl Rogers, Abraham Maslow	Reaching Full Potential	Humans have the potential for personal growth.
Evolutionary	Charles Darwin	Natural Selection	Natural selection favors behaviors that enhance reproductive success.

Perspective	Contributors	Subject Matter	Basic Premise
Biological	**Roger Sperry, David Hubel, Torsten Wiesel**	Physiological Bases of behavior	Behavior and the mind are best understood by examining bodily structures and biochemical processes.
Cognitive	**Jean Piaget, Noam Chomsky**	Thoughts, Memory, Language, Problem-Solving	Examines how people think, remember, process information, and use language.
Biopsychosocial		Combining Biological, Psychological, and Social	A multi-faceted approach that combines B, P, and S
Sociocultural	**Phillip Zimbardo, Stanley Milgram, Solomon Asche,**	Culture and Environment	Studies on how culture and environment shape behavior

An important debate that persists throughout psychology is called <u>nurture versus nature.</u> To what extent is who we are as people due to our environment (nurture) or our biology and genes (nature)?

1.2 What are the methods psychologist use to study the mind and behavior?

Basic Research	Research to advance knowledge without consideration of practical applications.
Applied Research	Studies conducted to solve real-world problems
Psychometrics	Assigning numbers to behaviors, thoughts, and other psychological phenomena
Case Studies	Studying one or a few people in great depth
Naturalistic Observation	Watch and record everyday behavior in natural settings.
Survey	A study in which researchers select a group of participants from a population and data about or opinions from those participants are collected, measured, and analyzed.
Correlational Research	Study the relationship between variables or how well they can predict one another.
Experimentation	- A series of observations conducted by researchers under controlled conditions to study a relationship and to draw causal inferences about that relationship - An experiment involves the manipulation of an independent variable, measuring a dependent variable, and exposing various participants to one or more of the conditions researchers are studying. - Selection of participants and their random assignment to conditions also are necessary for experiments.
Cross-Sectional	Comparing people or groups of people of different ages at one point in time
Longitudinal	Comparing the same people over time
Meta-Analysis	Combining the results of many studies on the same topic into one

Why is there a need for psychological science?

Hindsight Bias	Believing that we know something only after the event occurs. "I knew it all along."
Overconfidence	Believing that we know more than we actually do.
Illusory Correlations	The appearance of a relationship when one does not exist

1.3 What is the experimental method, and how does it work?

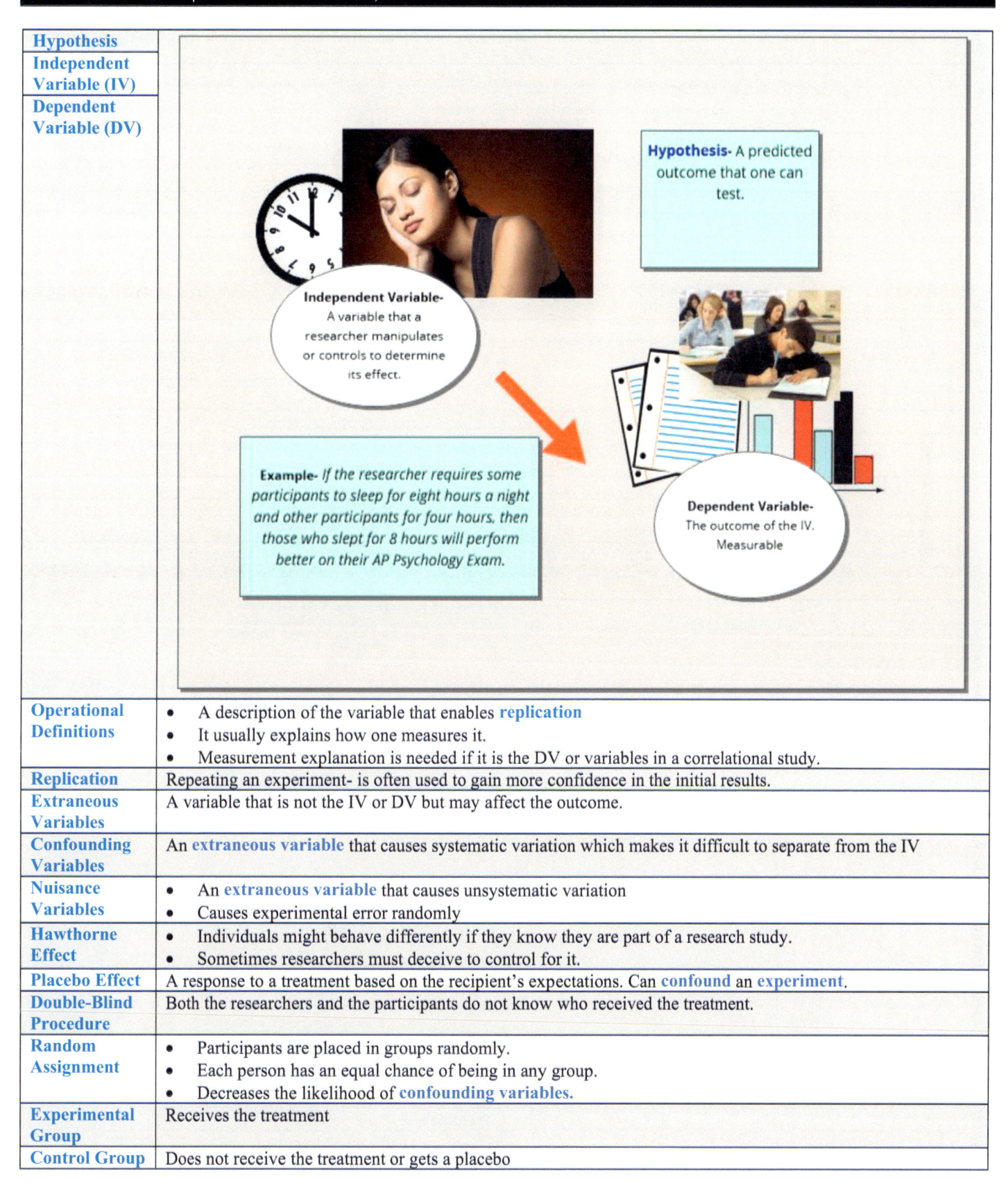

Hypothesis **Independent Variable (IV)** **Dependent Variable (DV)**	*Hypothesis-* A predicted outcome that one can test. *Independent Variable-* A variable that a researcher manipulates or controls to determine its effect. *Example-* If the researcher requires some participants to sleep for eight hours a night and other participants for four hours, then those who slept for 8 hours will perform better on their AP Psychology Exam. *Dependent Variable-* The outcome of the IV. Measurable
Operational Definitions	• A description of the variable that enables replication • It usually explains how one measures it. • Measurement explanation is needed if it is the DV or variables in a correlational study.
Replication	Repeating an experiment- is often used to gain more confidence in the initial results.
Extraneous Variables	A variable that is not the IV or DV but may affect the outcome.
Confounding Variables	An extraneous variable that causes systematic variation which makes it difficult to separate from the IV
Nuisance Variables	• An extraneous variable that causes unsystematic variation • Causes experimental error randomly
Hawthorne Effect	• Individuals might behave differently if they know they are part of a research study. • Sometimes researchers must deceive to control for it.
Placebo Effect	A response to a treatment based on the recipient's expectations. Can confound an experiment.
Double-Blind Procedure	Both the researchers and the participants do not know who received the treatment.
Random Assignment	• Participants are placed in groups randomly. • Each person has an equal chance of being in any group. • Decreases the likelihood of confounding variables.
Experimental Group	Receives the treatment
Control Group	Does not receive the treatment or gets a placebo

Study Tip- **Retrieval Practice**: Cover up the definitions and try to explain each one to your stuffed animal, pet, friend, or family member. Uncover to check if you are correct.

1.4 What are the strengths and weaknesses of the research methods?

Case Studies	
strengths	weaknesses
<ul><li>Dig deep</li><li>Describe rare phenomena</li><li>Provide areas for further exploration</li></ul>	<ul><li>Time-consuming</li><li>Subjects may not be representative</li><li>Cannot prove causality</li></ul>

Naturalistic Observation	
strengths	weaknesses
<ul><li>Reduces Hawthorne Effect</li><li>Real behavior</li><li>Describes behavior</li></ul>	<ul><li>Does not explain</li><li>No control</li><li>Cannot prove causality</li></ul>

Surveys	
strengths	weaknesses
<ul><li>Inexpensive</li><li>Study many variables</li></ul>	<ul><li>Hard to obtain a representative sample of a population- it needs random sampling</li><li>Wording effects</li><li>Cannot prove causality</li></ul>

Representative Sample	Selecting participants so that the sample accurately reflects the entire population
Population	The total number of individuals in a given area
Random Sampling	Every person in a population has the same probability of being selected. It helps make the sample representative of the population by reducing bias.
Wording Effects	The way researchers write a question can influence how a participant answers it.

Correlational Studies	
strengths	weaknesses
<ul><li>Indicates the strength and relationship between variables</li><li>Can happen outside a lab</li></ul>	<ul><li>**Correlation does not necessarily mean causation.**</li><li>Illusory correlations</li><li>Third variable</li></ul>

Experimentation	
Strengths	Weaknesses
<ul><li>**Can demonstrate causality**</li></ul>	<ul><li>Possible ethical implications</li><li>Type I and Type II Errors</li><li>Cannot control all variables</li></ul>

Cross-Sectional		Longitudinal	
Strengths	**Weaknesses**	**Strengths**	**Weaknesses**
Can compare different ages	Difficult to prove causality	Eliminates environmental differences	It takes a long time
	Environmental differences in age groups **confound**		Participants drop out- **attrition**

1.5 What statistical techniques do psychological researchers use?

Correlations

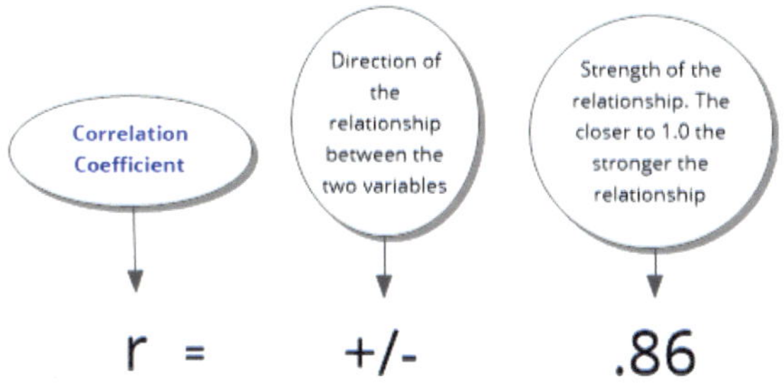

- Correlation Coefficient
- Direction of the relationship between the two variables
- Strength of the relationship. The closer to 1.0 the stronger the relationship

r = +/− .86

Scatterplots- graphical representation of correlations

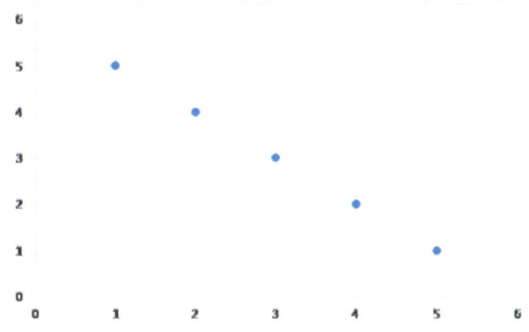

Perfect Negative Correlation r = -1.0

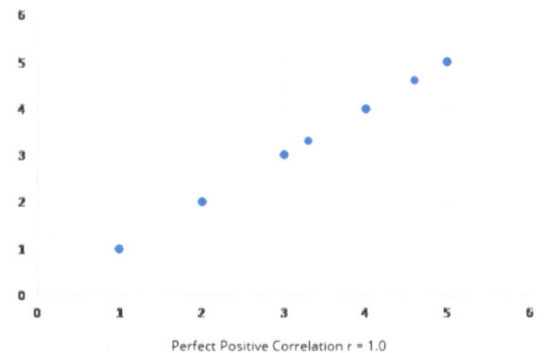

Perfect Positive Correlation r = 1.0

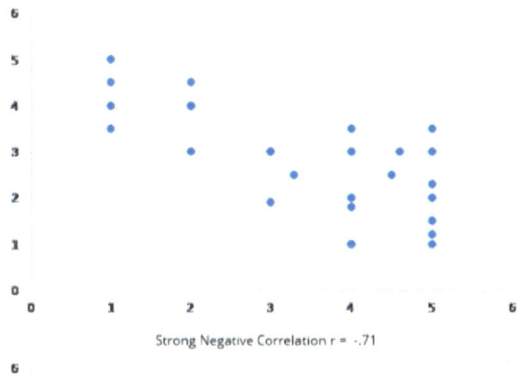

Strong Negative Correlation r = -.71

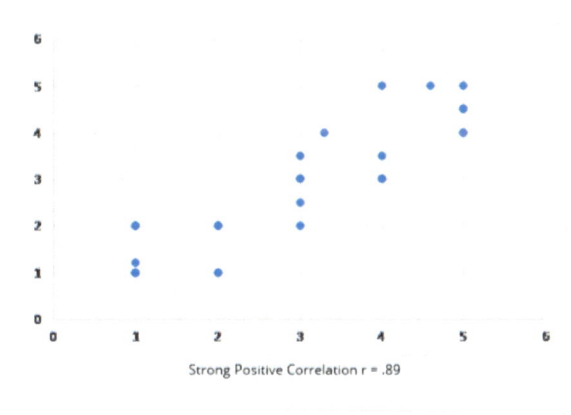

Strong Positive Correlation r = .89

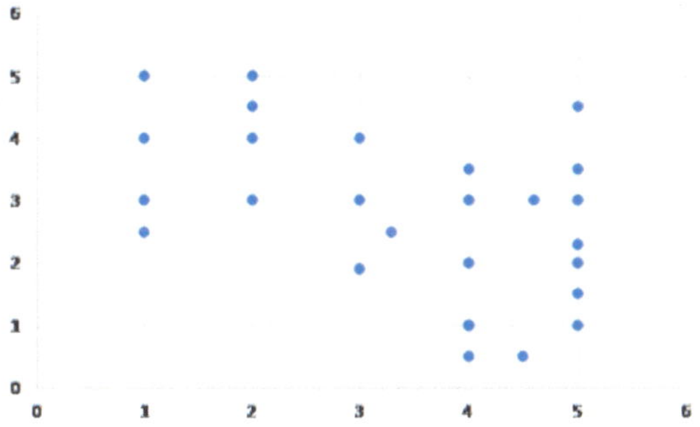

Moderate Negative Correlation r = -.48

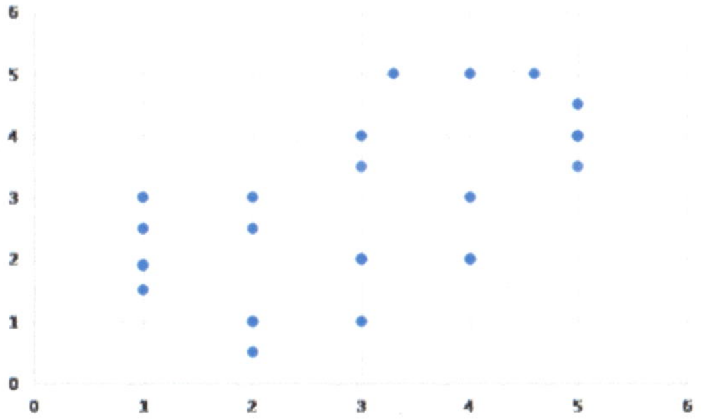

No Correlation r = 0.0

Moderate Positive Correlation r = .61

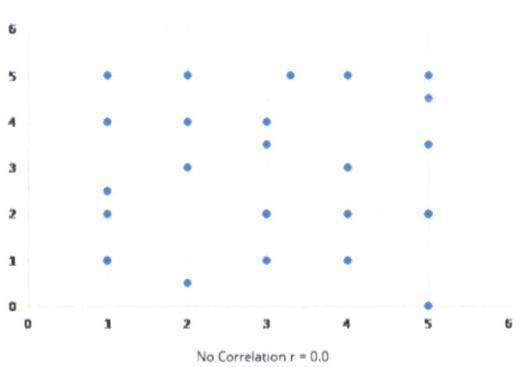

*** Positive is not necessarily bigger than negative. Positive and negative only indicate the direction of the relationship. Ex. r = − .7 is stronger than r = +.5 ***

Descriptive Statistics	• The main aspects of a data sample without inferring to a larger population • Usually, the mean, median, or mode
Central Tendency	The middle or center point of a set of scores
Mean	• The average • Sum of all scores divided by the number of scores. • Default measurement • Not used when there are extreme outliers and few scores.
Median	The midpoint of scores.
Mode	The most frequently occurring.
Range	Subtract the lowest score from the highest score.

Standard Deviation (SD)	• A measure of the variability of scores around the mean • A small SD means the scores are close to the mean. A large SD means they vary from the mean. • Often displayed as a bell curve

Inferential Statistics	People use them to determine what can be known about a population from the sample studied.
Statistical Significance	• Evaluation of the confidence that the change was not due to chance • Often set at 5% • Also called the p-value • Sample size impacts the significance • The larger the sample, the less likely the findings occurred by chance.
T-test	Statistical significance test that compares two conditions or groups
F-test (ANOVA)	Statistical significance test that compares more than two groups or conditions
Null Hypothesis	The assumption is that there is no difference between groups. Rejecting the null hypothesis means there was a difference.
Type I Error	Rejecting the null hypothesis when it was true
Type II Error	Failing to reject the null when it was not true

1.6 What are the ethical guidelines researchers must follow when conducting research?

American Psychological Association (APA)	Sets the guidelines for ethical research.
Informed Consent	• Prior approval to participate. • Often requires a signature of the participants.
Debriefing	Explain the true purpose of a study after completion.

Institutional Review Board (IRB)	• Must give prior approval
	• They consider:
	   o No undue harm (psychological, emotional, physical, economic, social, etc.)
	   o Confidentiality- Participants remain anonymous with no identifying information
	   o Cost-benefit analysis
	   o Deception is allowed

Institutional Animal Care and Use Committee (IACUC)	• Sets restrictions and gives approval for animal research
	• Guidelines:
	   o Use as few as needed to obtain valid results
	   o Can investigate infractions
	   o Researchers must ensure proper care
	   o Proper temperature
	   o Well fed
	   o Cages cleaned
	   o Holding rooms secured
	   o Must humanely sacrifice the animals

Unit 2- Biological Bases of Behavior (8-10% AP Exam Weighting)

2.1 How do heredity, environment, and evolution interact to shape behavior?

Biology	The study of living organisms.
Heredity	The study of how parents pass traits and genes to offspring
Heritability	The extent that genes can explain behavior.
Genes	The storage unit of information about an organism
The Theory Evolution	The gradual change in a population over many generations due to natural selection
Natural Selection	<ul><li>Environmental factors eliminate those individuals who cannot adapt and thus gradually eliminate maladaptive characteristics.</li><li>Those who have characteristics that help them survive are more likely to produce offspring with those same characteristics.</li><li>Also, called the survival of the fittest.</li><li>It causes populations to evolve over many generations.</li></ul>
Charles Darwin	British naturalists who co-created the theory of evolution by studying animal populations. He wrote On the Origin of Species

A method psychologists use for heredity research is twin studies. Identical twins share more genetic material than fraternal twins, which share more genetic material than siblings, which share more than non-related people.

2.2 How does the endocrine system affect behavior?

Endocrine System	Chemical system that sends slow-moving messages through the bloodstream.
Hormones	Chemical messengers of the endocrine system

Body Part	Hormone	Function
Hypothalamus of the Brain		Controls the pituitary gland
Pituitary Gland	Many	It affects other glands and regulates growth
Thyroid Gland	Thyroid Hormone	Affects metabolism
Adrenal Gland	Epinephrine (adrenaline) and Norepinephrine	Triggers the flight or fight response
Pineal Gland	Melatonin	Helps regulate circadian rhythm.
Parathyroid	Thyroid Hormone	It affects the level of calcium and phosphate in the blood
Pancreas		Regulates the level of sugar in the blood
Testis	Testosterone, sperm	Male sex hormones.
Ovary	Estrogen, egg cells	Female sex hormones.

Parts of the Endocrine System

HYPOTHALAMUS - connects the nervous system and endocrine system; controls hormones from the central nervous sytem

PITUITARY GLAND - monitors and regulates growth hormones; also controls reproductive glands

PINEAL GLAND - produces melatonin that regulates sleep

THYROID - regulates metabolism and use of energy

ADRENAL GLAND - produces hormones that help regulate metabolism and other body functions

PANCREAS - produces hormones that regulate blood glucose

OVARY (IN FEMALES) - produces estrogen that controls female puberty and progesterone that manages fertility

TESTIS (IN MALES) - produces testosterone that controls male puberty and ability to produce sperm

2.3 What are the classifications of the nervous system?

Study Tip- Hierarchical Organization- Memorizing items in categories and subcategories helps storage and retrieval of the items when taking a test (See "The Nervous System" below).

The Nervous System

- **Central Nervous System**
  - The Brain
  - Spinal Cord
    - Reflexes
      - Motor Neurons
      - Sensory Neurons
      - Interneurons
    - Information Highway

- **Peripheral Nervous System**
  - Somatic Nervous System
    - Nerves to voluntary muscles → Efferent → Outgoing
    - Nerves to Sensory Receptors → Afferent → Incoming
  - Automatic Nervous System
    - Sympathetic Division → Mobilizes Bodily Resources → accelerate heartbeat, raise blood pressure, slow your digestion,
    - Parasympathetic Division → Conserves Bodily Resources → decreasing heartbeat, lowering blood sugar

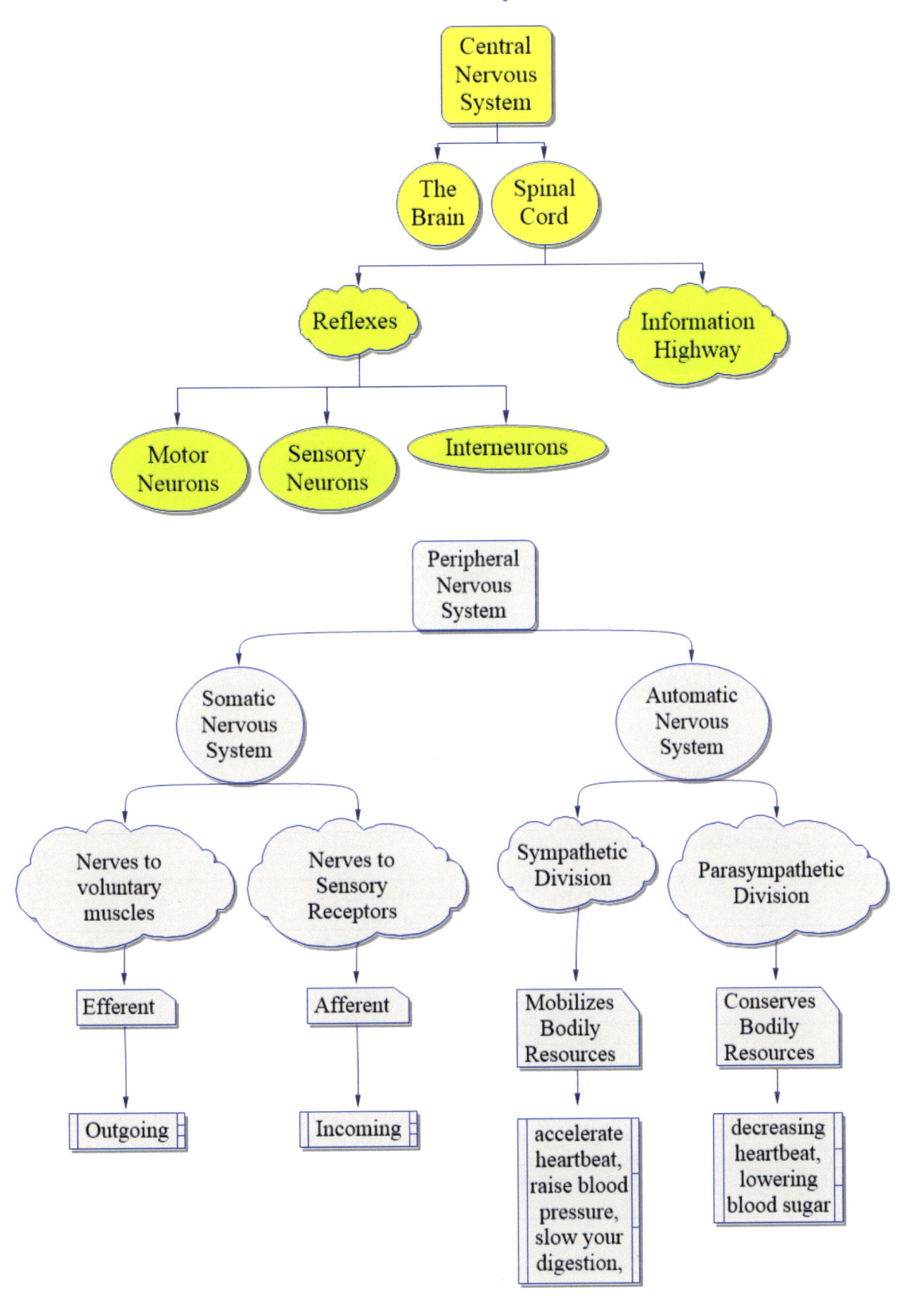

2.4 What is a neuron, its parts, and what are their functions?

Neuron	Cellular units of the nervous system (nerve cells)
Sensory Neuron	A neuron that receives information from the environment
Motor Neuron	A neuron that connects to muscle fibers
Interneuron	A connector neuron. Often found in the spinal cord.
Reflex	An automatic response to a stimulus that involves the sensory neurons to interneurons and back to the motor neurons before the brain registers the stimulus

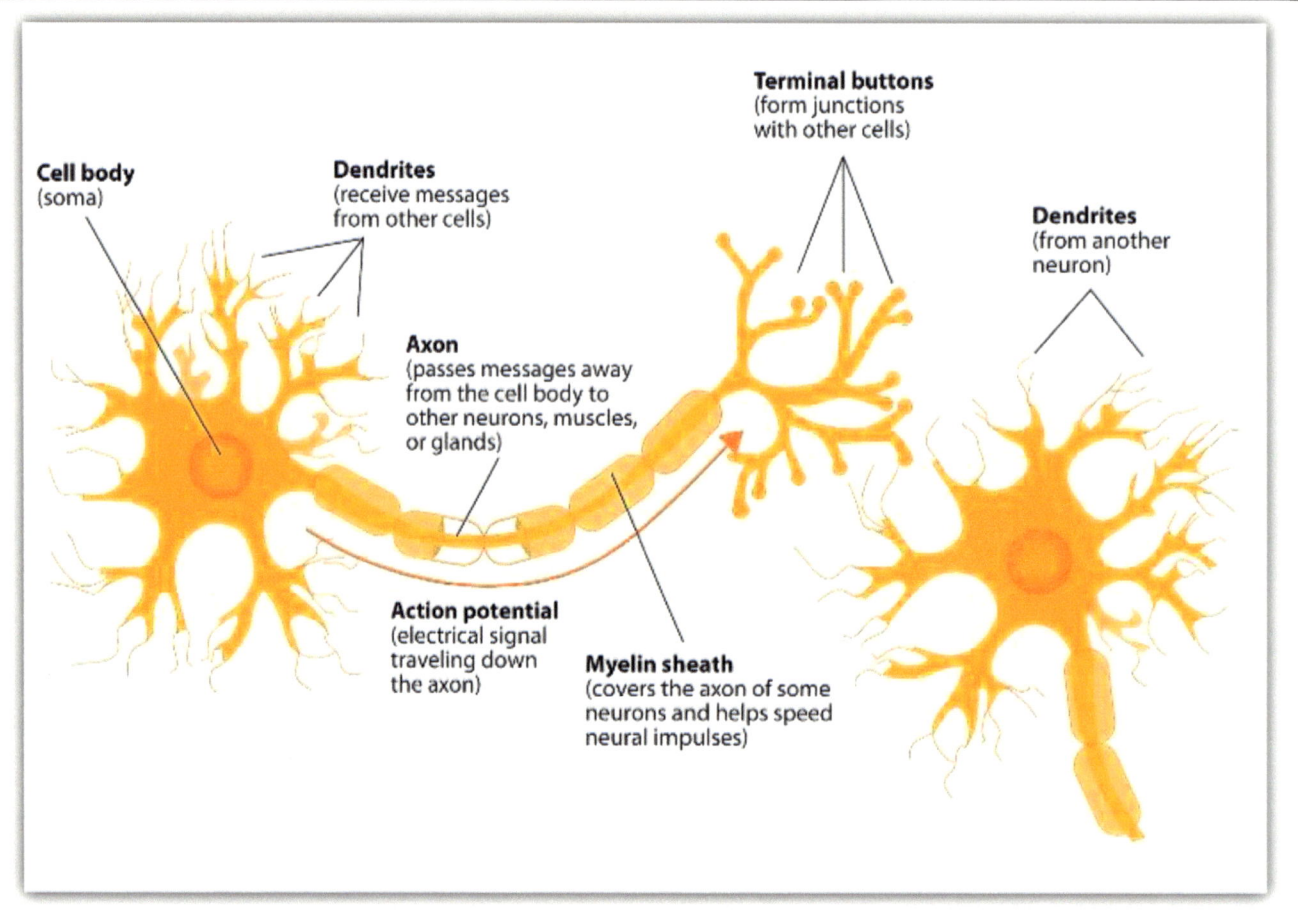

Jennifer Walinga, Components of neuron, CC BY-SA 4.0

Dendrites	Extension of the cell body that receives messages
Cell Body (Soma)	The part of the neuron that contains the nucleus.
Axon	• Extension of a nerve cell that carries electrical messages • Axons can travel long distances throughout the body.
Myelin Sheath	• The insulating layer surrounding the axon that increases the speed of transmission • A breakdown of the myelin sheath is a cause of multiple sclerosis.
Terminal Branches	Discharges chemical neurotransmitters into the synapse
Action Potential	Neural firing. A change in electrical charge takes place in the axon.
Resting Potential	The cell is at rest. -70 MV inside the axon.
Threshold for Excitation	• Stimulus intensity is significant enough to make a neuron fire. • Or when the excitatory neurotransmitters exceed the inhibitory.
Refractory Period	A period of inactivity after a cell fired. It will not respond to stimuli.
Gray Matter	Cell bodies
White Matter	Axons and myelin sheath

Neurons have an all-or-none-response; if a stimulus is powerful, only the number of neurons firing will increase, not their speed.

Synapse

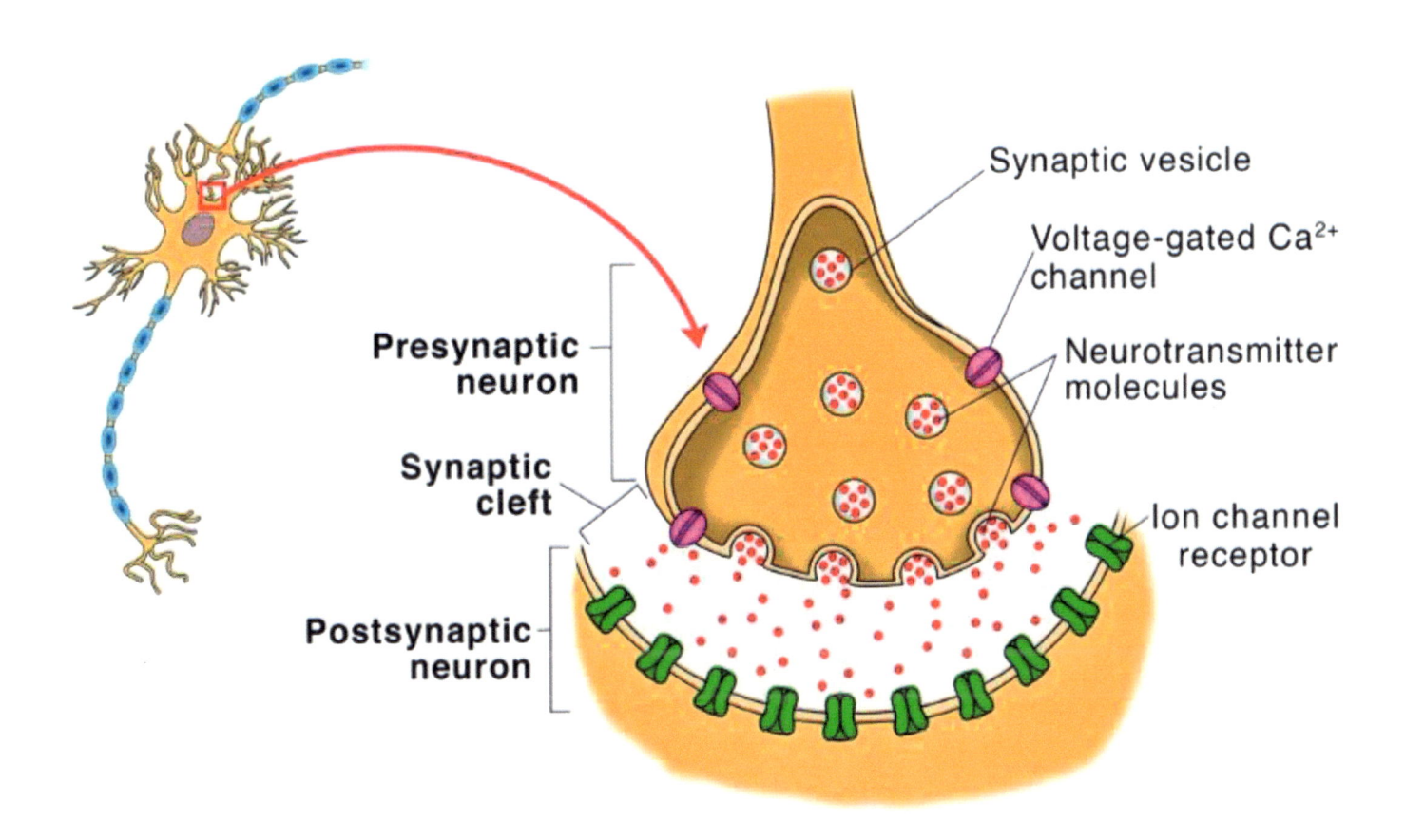

(ScienceFacts.Net/Synapse, 2021)

Synapse or Synaptic Gap	• The space between a sending and receiving neuron. • Release of neurotransmitters from the sending neuron.
Synaptic Vesicle	Spherical molecules that contain neurotransmitters
Neurotransmitters	Chemical messengers
Ion Channel	Selective or gated openings in a cell membrane

A Few Neurotransmitters and Their Function(s)	
Acetylcholine (Ach)	• Enables muscle memory, action, and learning • Ach deteriorates in people with Alzheimer's disease.
Dopamine	• Influences movement and emotion • Found in pleasure centers of the brain. • Excess linked to Schizophrenia • Too little linked to Parkinson's Disease
Serotonin	• It affects mood (happiness), hunger, and sleep • Undersupply linked to depression
GABA (gamma-aminobutyric acid)	• Inhibitory- prevents neural firing • Involved in memory • Undersupply linked to seizures
Glutamate	• Excitatory- helps neural firing • Oversupply can overstimulate the brain causing headaches and seizures. • Some foods have MSG, an artificial additive

2.5 How do drugs influence neural firing?

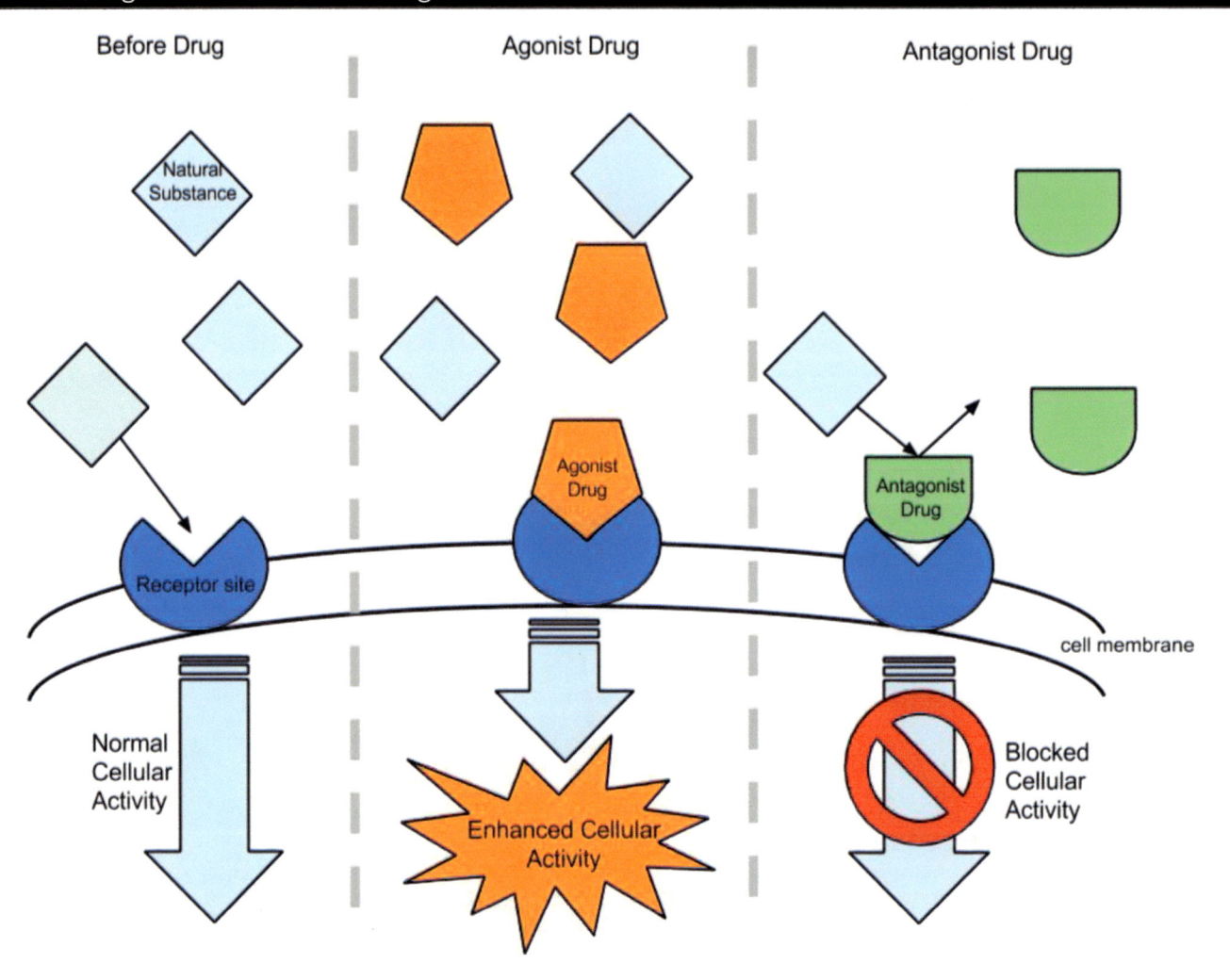

Dolleyj (https://commons.wikimedia.org/wiki/File:Agonist_&_Antagonist.jpg), „Agonist & Antagonist", https://creativecommons.org/licenses/by-sa/3.0/legalcode

Agonist	• A chemical or drug that binds to the receptor site of a neuron.
	• Produces an effect similar to a neurotransmitter.
	• Often the body stops producing the neurotransmitter if the drug/chemical is present.
Antagonist	• A chemical or drug that binds to the receptor site of a neuron.
	• Similar enough to attach, but not similar enough to trigger an **action potential.**
	• Blocks **neurotransmitters** from attaching.
Reuptake Inhibitors	Block the sending **neuron** from reabsorption of **neurotransmitters,** keeping them in the **synaptic gap** longer.

2.6 What are the brain's structures and their corresponding functions?

Brainstem	The Medulla , Pons, Reticular Formation, and Thalamus	
Medulla and Medulla Oblongata	Breathing, heartbeat, and blood pressure	
Pons	Helps coordinate movements	
Reticular Formation	Arousal, alertness, sleep, passing signals from the spine to the higher parts of the brain	
Moruzzi and Magoun	• Electrically stimulated a cat's **reticular formation,** and it was highly alert. • Severed the **reticular formation,** and it lapsed into a coma.	
Thalamus	Receives sensory input (except smell) and routes them to the higher brain regions.	

Belomaad (https://commons.wikimedia.org/wiki/File:Basic_structures_of_the_brain_highlighted.png), „Basic structures of the brain highlighted, "https://creativecommons.org/licenses/by-sa/4.0/legalcode

Limbic System	• The emotional brain, some memory functions
	• Hypothalamus, Nucleus Accumbens, Pituitary Gland, Amygdala, Hippocampus, Cerebellum

	Hypothalamus	• Appetite and thirst • Ventromedial- stimulation makes one full (satiated). A lesion does the opposite. • Lateral- stimulation makes one hungry. A lesion does the opposite.
	Nucleus Accumbens	• Front of the hypothalamus • Olds and Milner • Reward center • Dopamine releases for activities such as eating, drinking, and sex
	Pituitary Gland	• Master gland • Growth hormone • Endocrine System
	Amygdala	Fear, fight or flight response
	Hippocampus	• Processes declarative memory for long-term storage • It is not the location of stored memories.
	Cerebellum	It helps maintain balance and coordinate muscle movements

Cerebral Cortex or Neocortex or Cerebrum	Section of gray matter on top of the brain is involved in higher-level thinking such as language, problem-solving, perception, and planning.

Frontal Lobe	• Motor functions Planning, judgment, problem-solving, decision-making, organization, inhibitory control, abstraction, logic

	Motor Cortex	Part of the frontal lobe that directs and controls movement.
	Phineas Gage	• Famous case study. • A tamping rod passed through his frontal lobe. He lost the ability to control his emotions.

Parietal Lobe	• Somatosensory activities. • Some aspects of speech and language

	Sensory Cortex	• Receives messages from sensory neurons • Determines the location of the body that received the stimuli.
	Penfield Map	Foerster and Penfield electrically stimulated awake patients to determine which body parts responded to various places in the parietal lobe. (see image below)

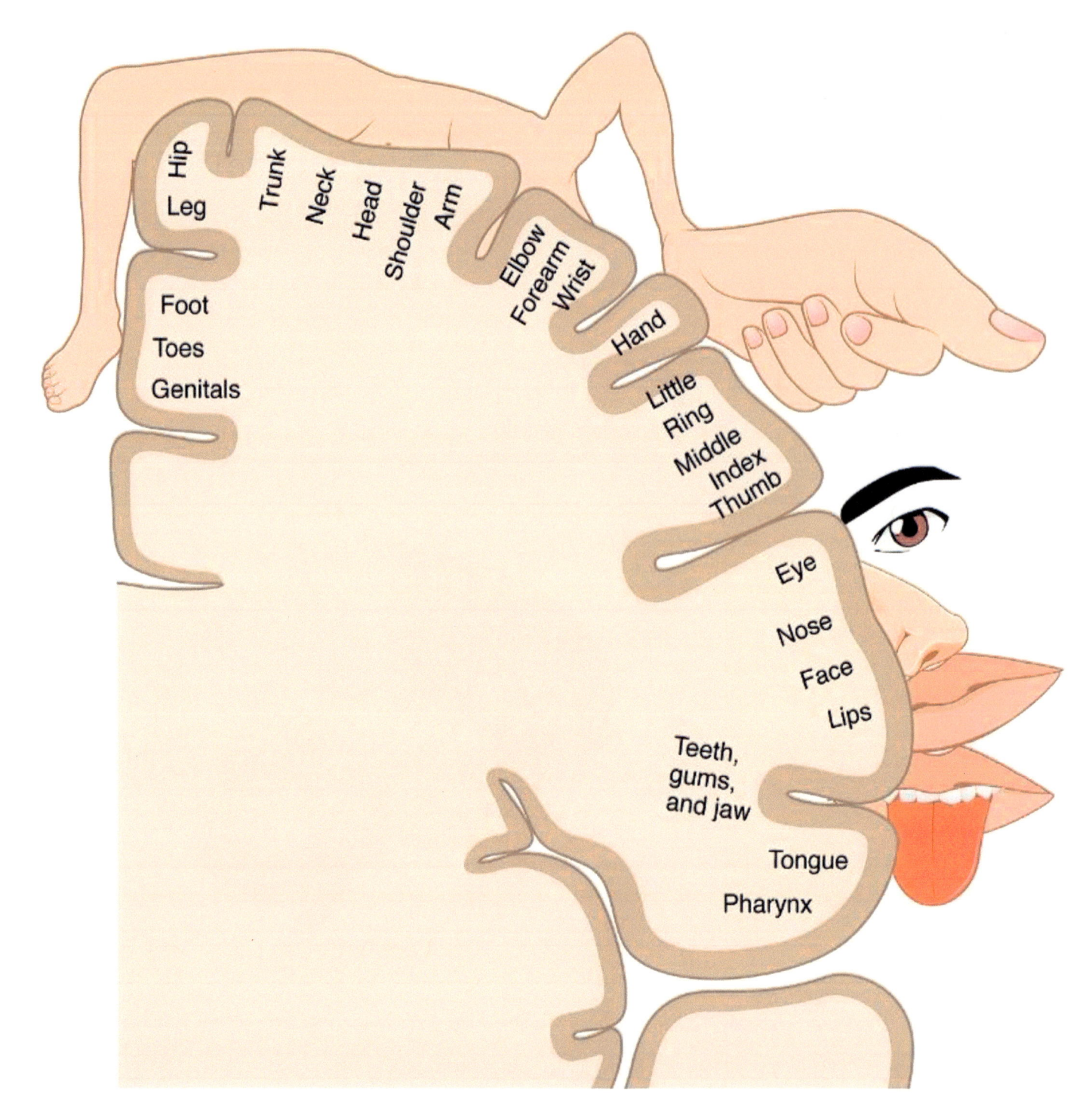

OpenStax College, 1421 Sensory Homunculus, CC BY 3.0

Temporal Lobe	Involved in many auditory tasks
Auditory Cortex	Receives and processes sound

Occipital Lobe	Receives and processes visual stimuli
Visual Cortex	Section of the occipital lobe.
Association Areas	Any area of the cerebral cortex that does not involve sensory or motor perceptions

Broca's Area	Production of speech	
Wernicke's Area	Interpretation of sounds	
Angular Gyrus	• Converts visual input to sound • Necessary for reading	

OpenStax College, 1605 Brocas and Wernickes Areas-02, CC BY 3.0

2.7 What tools do scientists use for examining the brain?

Autopsy	• Examining the brain of a dead person • Useful in case studies of extreme brain injury patients.
Lesions	Remove brain tissue and observe behavioral changes.
Electroencephalogram (EEG)	• The measure of brain electrical activity with sensors on top of the skull Good temporal resolution- fast • Poor spatial resolution- hard to measure lower brain regions or exact locations • Often used in sleep studies
Computed Tomography (CT or CAT Scan)	X-ray photographs of the brain
Positron Emission Tomography (PET)	Detects radioactive glucose consumption in the brain
Magnetic Resonance Imaging (MRI)	Generates images of the brain with powerful magnets
Functional Magnetic Resonance Imaging (fMRI)	• Generates successive images • Poor temporal resolution • Good spatial resolution • Expensive • Cannot observe the brain in natural settings
Electrocorticography (ECoG)	Electrodes are placed directly on the cerebral cortex to measure electrical activity.
Optogenetics	Use light to activate individual neurons.

Split-Brain Patients		• Roger Sperry and Michael Gazzaniga severed the corpus callosum in patients with epilepsy. • Patients seemed to have no side effects. • Upon examination, patients demonstrated an inability for the two hemispheres to communicate. • Ex. They could not verbally identify visual stimuli in the left visual field; could identify it with their left hand, but not their right hand.
	Corpus Callosum	Bundle of nerve fibers that connect the two hemispheres of the brain.

2.8 How does the brain adapt to its environment?

Neuroplasticity	• The ability of the nervous system to change, adapt, and rewire based on input from the environment. • Ex. Someone who is blind still has a visual cortex, so those neurons dedicate themselves to a new function such as hearing. • Ex. Piano players' sensory cortex for their fingers expands due to the use and sensitivity to touch.
Neural pruning	Excessive or redundant neural networks disconnect to make the brain more efficient.

What are the classifications of drugs, and how do they affect the brain?

Type	Pleasure	Negative After	Biology
Depressants- diminishing the activity of a body system.			
Alcohol	Initial high, relaxation, disinhibition	Depressed mood, organ damage	Slows the nervous system
Heroin	A rush of euphoria, relief from pain	Depressed physiology, agonizing withdrawal	The brain stops producing endorphins
Hallucinogen- produces a sensory effect without the stimuli			
LSD	Visual trip	Risk of panic	
Marijuana (THC)	Enhanced sensation, relaxation, time distortion	Impaired memory, lung damage if smoked	
Stimulants- excites the functional activity of a body system.			
Caffeine	Increased alertness	Insomnia, uncomfortable withdrawal	
Nicotine	Arousal and relaxation	Cancer, heart disease	-develop a tolerance -increased blood pressure
Cocaine	A rush of euphoria, energy	Cardiovascular stress, depressive crash	-blocks reuptake of dopamine, norepinephrine, and serotonin. -the body stops producing them
Methamphetamine	Euphoria, energy	Insomnia, seizures, irritability	-triggers the release of dopamine -the body stops producing it.
Ecstasy (MDMA)	Emotional elevation, disinhibition	Dehydration, depressed mood, impaired cognitive Function	-Triggers the release of serotonin and blocks its reuptake -can damage serotonin-producing neurons= depressed mood

Tolerance	Diminished effect of the drug. It requires more of it to receive the same effect.
Withdrawal	Symptoms after stopping using. Include cognitive, physiological, emotional, insomnia, and behavioral.
Addiction	Physiological or psychological dependence on a drug

2.9 What is consciousness?

Consciousness	Awareness of ourselves and our environment

Sleep Cycle

Stage	Characteristics	Brain Waves
Awake		Alpha Waves
NREM-1	Hypnogogic Sensations- hallucinations without storylines.	Alpha and Theta Waves
NREM-2	Transitional stage between light and deep	Sleep Spindles, Theta Waves
NREM-3	deep sleep, night terrors, sleepwalking	Delta Waves
Rapid Eye Movement (REM)	dreaming, sleep paralysis, paradoxical sleep, sympathetic nervous system Arousal	• Fast and irregular • Beta Waves • The brainstem blocks messages from the motor cortex.

What are altered states of consciousness?

Spontaneous	Physiological	Psychological
daydreaming	hallucinations	hypnosis
dreaming	orgasms	meditation
drowsiness	food deprivation	
	oxygen deprivation	

What are our biological rhythms?

Circadian Rhythm	• 24-hour cycle of wake and sleep • Body temperature changes • Changes in **melatonin** levels • It is influenced by many factors such as sunlight, stimulants, food, etc.
Menstrual Cycle	• The 28-day cycle of **estrogen** production, **ovulation**, and **menstruation**
Sleep Cycle	• 90-minute cycle with changes in brain patterns. • Typically- 1,2,3,2,1, REM

Sleep Cycle

Stage	Characteristics	Brain Waves
Awake		**Alpha Waves**
NREM-1	**Hypnogogic Sensations**- hallucinations without storylines.	**Alpha and Theta Waves**
NREM-2	Transitional stage between light and deep	**Sleep Spindles, Theta Waves**
NREM-3	deep sleep, night terrors, sleepwalking	**Delta Waves**
Rapid Eye Movement (REM)	**dreaming, sleep paralysis, paradoxical sleep, sympathetic nervous system** Arousal	• Fast and irregular • **Beta Waves** • **The brainstem** blocks messages from the **motor cortex.**

Why do we sleep?

1. Evolutionary- sleep protected from predators.
2. Sleep repairs brain tissue- destroys **free radicals** accumulated during the day.
3. Help with **memory storage.**
4. Growth- **pituitary gland** releases growth **hormones** during sleep.

Why do we dream?

1. **Psychoanalytic-** Freud's Theory
   a. **Manifest Content**- Remembered storyline
   b. **Latent Content**- Hidden meaning of the symbols
2. **Information Processing**-Dreams help us sort out the day's events, problems, and memories.
3. **Physiological Function**- preserve neural pathways.
4. **Activation- Synthesis Theory**- The **brainstem** randomly generates neural impulses. Areas such as the **visual** and **auditory cortices** fire randomly. The dreamer weaves the neural impulses into a story.
5. **Cognitive Development**- Dreams reflect one's cognitive development.

What are the major sleep disorders?

Insomnia	Difficulty falling asleep or staying asleep.
Narcolepsy	Brief and uncontrollable attacks of sleep during the daytime
Sleep Apnea	• Brief moments when one stops breathing during sleep • No complete **sleep cycle**. • They are often fatigued during the day. • Treatment often requires a **CPAP** machine.
Sleep Walking	• Usually occurs during stage 3. • Often outgrow it.
Night Terrors	• More intense than nightmares. • It does not occur during REM • They do not remember the cause • Most often in children. Usually, outgrow it.

Unit 3- Sensation and Perception (6-8% AP Exam Weighting)

Sensation	Receiving information through the senses.
Perception	The process of organizing and interpreting stimuli into meaningful knowledge

3.1 What are the principles of sensation?

Absolute Threshold	The amount of stimulation needed to trigger awareness in 50% of the trials
Subliminal	<ul><li>Stimuli that are below the absolute or difference threshold</li><li>Stimulus is present but unnoticeable.</li></ul>
Difference Threshold	<ul><li>The smallest amount of noticeable difference between two stimuli in 50% of trials</li><li>Also called the just noticeable difference or JND.</li></ul>
Weber's Law	<ul><li>Ernst Heinrich Weber</li><li>Mathematical formula</li><li>The difference threshold is proportional to the intensity of the stimulus.</li><li>If the intensity of the stimulus increases, so will the JND.</li></ul>
Signal Detection Theory	External noises and expectations impact the absolute threshold.
Sensory Adaptation	Reduced responsiveness in the sensory systems after a prolonged or repeated stimulation
Transduction	The process of changing a sensory stimulus to an electrical signal
Bottom-Up Processing	Processing incoming stimuli by their parts to recognize, interpret or categorize.
Top-Down Processing	Using previous experiences, knowledge, or hypotheses about incoming stimuli, recognize, interpret, or categorize.

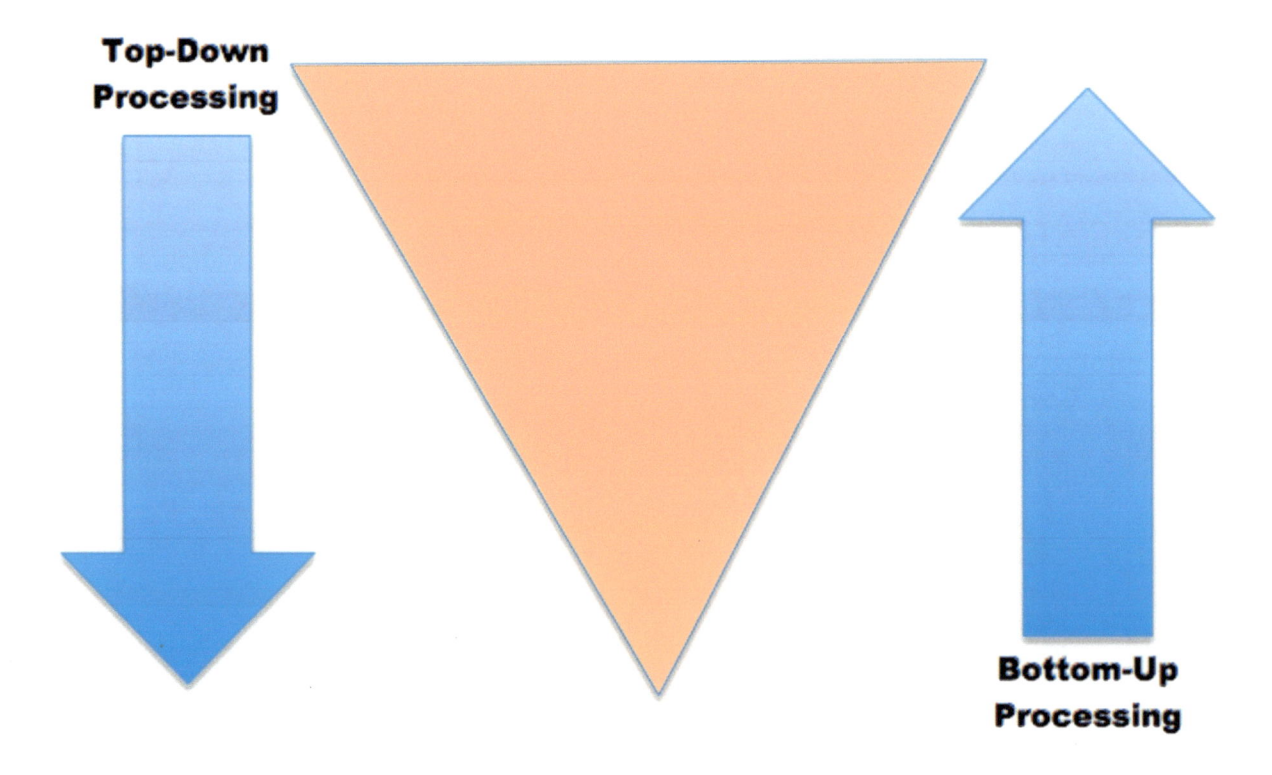

Khikida, Top-Down Bottom-Up Processing, CC BY-SA 4.0

3.2 How does our mind organize and interpret sensory information?

Gestalt- integrating elements to create a whole configuration not possessed by the individual parts.	
Proximity	Organizing objects that are close to each other into a group
Similarity	Organizing objects with similar qualities into a group
Symmetry	Mirrorlike on either side of a center point or line.
Closure	Perceiving incomplete forms as complete by closing gaps
Continuity	Perceiving objects as smooth and with unbroken contours even if it is not in reality
Connection	Grouping objects together that are connected.
Figure-Ground	• Perceiving one object as the foreground that stands out from the indistinct background • Illusions can make switch the figure and ground.

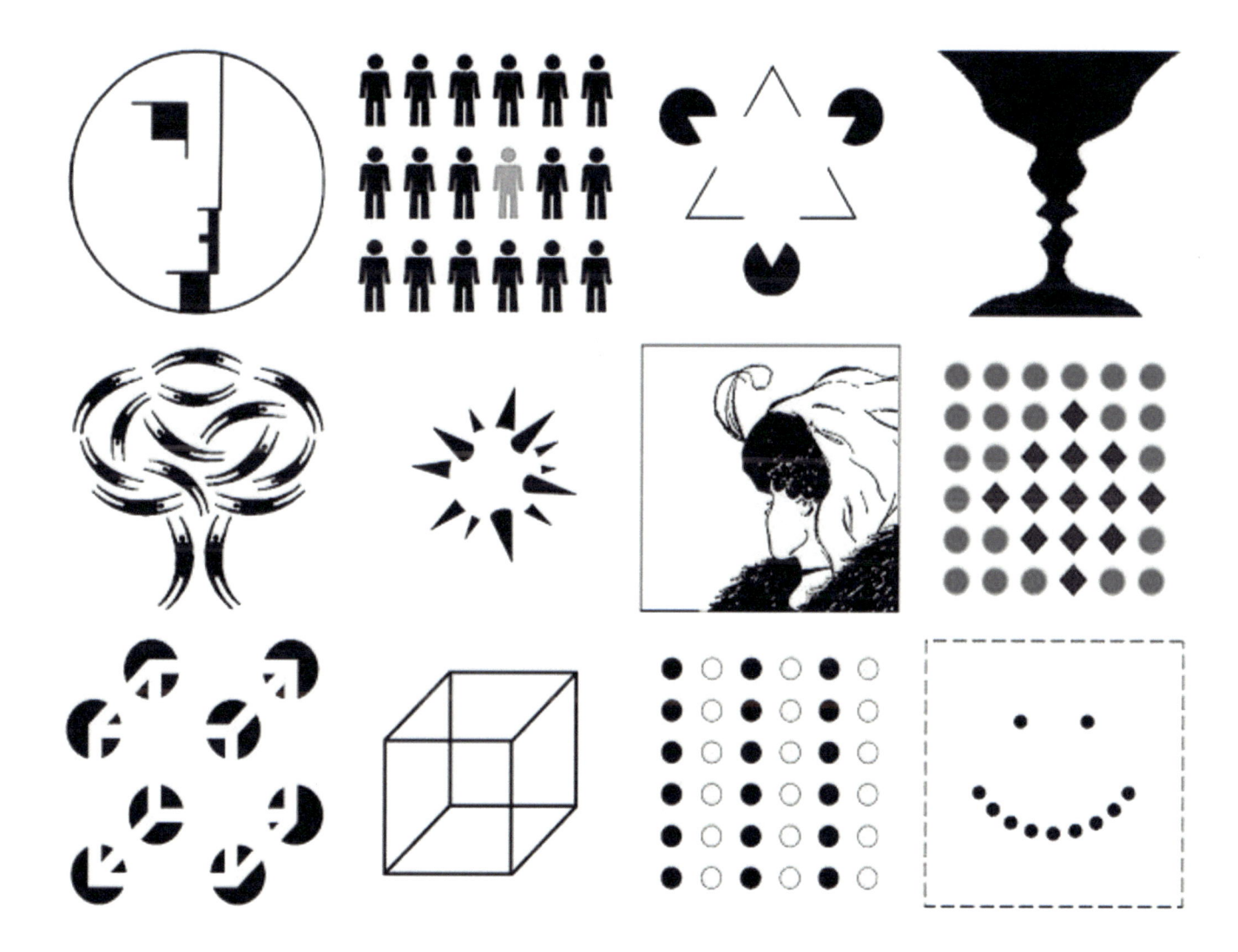

Akermariano, Gestalt Principles Composition, CC BY-SA 3.0

How does experience and culture influence perception?

Perceptual Set	A schema that influences the way a person perceives
Context Effect	Context can alter the way a person perceives. Cultural context changes schemas.
Schema	A collection of knowledge about a concept that shapes how one perceives

How is depth perception experienced?

Depth Perception	The ability to perceive in three dimensions with a distance between the observer and the object
Visual Cliff	<ul><li>**Gibson and Walk**</li><li>Apparatus to test depth perception nature versus nurture</li><li>Reluctance to crawl to the mother indicates **depth perception.**</li><li>Infants at six months will not cross</li></ul> From Gibson and Walk (1960). Copyright 1960 Nature Publishing Group., NIH visual cliff experiment, CC BY 4.0
Binocular Depth Cues	Using information from both eyes to determine the depth of an object
Convergence	<ul><li>When the eyes rotate inward toward an object to help determine its depth.</li><li>The closer the object, the larger the angle it creates.</li></ul> I, Sbitzer, Binocular disparity 2D, CC BY-SA 3.0
Retinal Disparity	The difference between the right and left retinal images is compared by the brain and fused into one image with depth.

23

	Monocular Depth Cues- Using information from one eye to determine depth.	
Relative Size	When two objects are similar in size, the one that casts a smaller retinal image, the viewer perceives it as further away.	
Interposition	When an object obstructs the view of another, the viewer perceives the one that is blocked as further away.	
Relative Clarity	When an object is hazy, it is perceived as further away because usually, it indicates that the object passed through more light to reach the retinas.	
Texture Gradient	When object texture becomes more indistinct, the viewer perceives it as further away.	
Relative Height	When an object is higher in the visual field, the viewer perceives it as further away.	Pk0001, Wundt illusion vertical-horizontal illusion, CC BY-SA 4.0 *The horizontal and vertical lines are the same length.*
Relative Motion	• Objects closer to a fixation point move faster and in the opposite direction. • Objects beyond the fixation point move in the same direction	
Linear Perspective	Parallel lines converge at a point on the horizon as the distance away from the viewer increases.	

3.3 What are the structures and functions of the parts of the eye?

Cornea	Protective outer layer
Iris	The muscle around the pupil
Pupil	Adjustable opening
Lens	• Changes the focus of light toward the retina • The process is called accommodation.
Optic Nerve	Sends the messages to the brain
Retina	• Multi-neuron surface at the back of the eye • Two types of receptor cells: rods and cones
Blindspot	• People cannot see the light that lands on this retina spot. • No receptor cells on this part of the retina • Place where the optic nerve meets the retina • The brain fills in, and the other eye compensates
Fovea	In the retina. Central focus area. High concentration of cones.

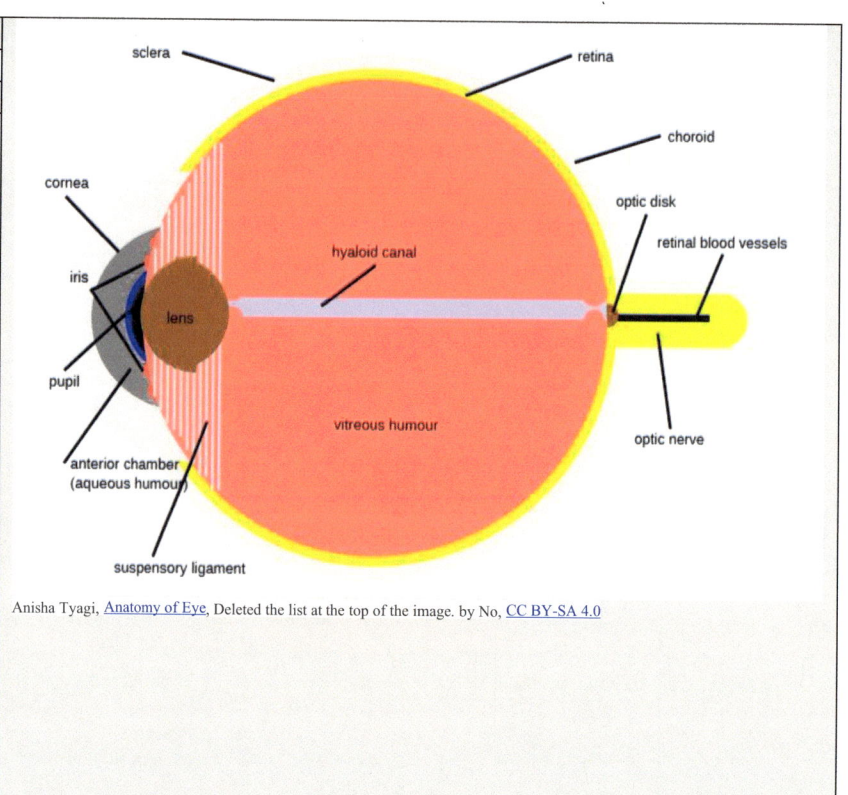

Anisha Tyagi, Anatomy of Eye, Deleted the list at the top of the image. by No, CC BY-SA 4.0

Cones	• Detect color • Detail • Sensitive in daylight • More in the fovea
Rods	• Detect the brightness of the light • Less fine detail • Sensitive in darkness • More outside the fovea • Peripheral vision	•

Christine Blume, Corrado Garbazza & Manuel Spitschan, Overview of the retina photoreceptors (a), CC BY 4.0

How do the eyes see?

Phototransduction	• Conversion of light energy into neural impulses • Occurs in the retina	
Light	Electromagnetic waves	
Wavelengths	• Distance from one peak to another.	

25

	• Determines hue (color, i.e., red, blue, green) • Short wavelength=bluish colors • Long wavelength=red colors	
Amplitude	• Height of the wave • Determines intensity (brightness)	Geoff Ruth, Crest trough wavelength amplitude, CC BY-SA 3.0
Acuity	Sharpness and clarity	
Nearsightedness	• Only see near objects clearly • Light falls short of the retina	
Farsightedness	• Only see far objects clearly • Light projects too far past the retina	
Feature Detectors	• Hubel and Wiesel • Found certain neural networks respond to only specific features of what we see. • Shape, color, depth, movement, form, angle, postures, gaze	
Parallel Processing	The brain processes a lot of information simultaneously.	

How do the eyes and brain determine color?

Young-Helmholtz Trichromatic Theory	• Three types of cones detect light • Each is sensitive to Red, Green, or Blue light waves • Combinations produce other colors
Opponent-Process Theory	• Color is processed by its opponent's color • Red-Green, Blue-Yellow, Black-White • Some cells are excited by blue and inhibited by yellow and vice versa.
Color Adding	• Adding wavelengths together • All colors together produce white light.
Color Subtracting	• Mixing colors on the surface of an object subtract wavelengths that reflect off it and reach the retina. • Mixing all the colors subtracts all the colors reflected, resulting in the perception of black.
Color Constancy	The ability to perceive the same color under different conditions of illumination
Color Blindness	• The inability to discriminate between specific colors/hues • The most common form affects the red and green cones in the retina. • Rare for someone to see no color.

3.4 How does the mind perceive visual input, and how do those perceptions create illusions?

Visual Capture	Vision overrides and dominates the other senses when a conflict arises.
Perceptual Constancy	• An object's properties are perceived as unchanged even though the stimulus did change. • Brightness constancy, color constancy, shape constancy, size constancy, lightness constancy,

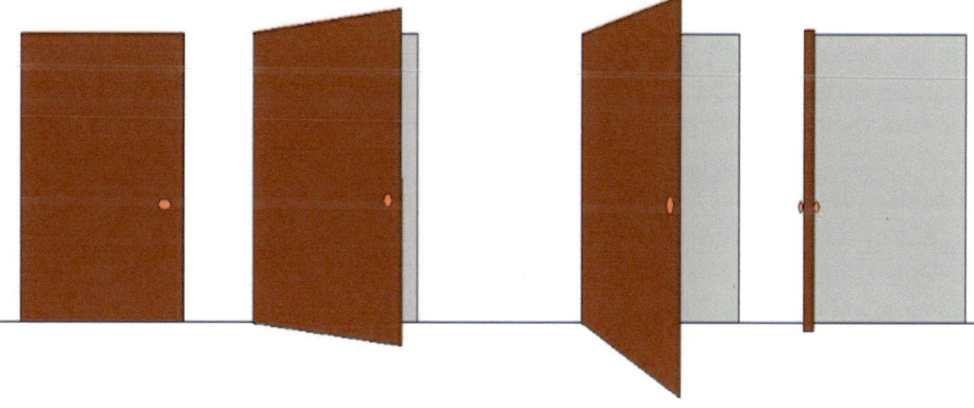

*The image above demonstrates shape constancy. The door is perceived as a rectangle even though as it opens, the shape changes.

Phi Phenomenon	The illusion of movement when one light turns on then off, followed by a nearby light turning on then off.
Size-Distance Relationship	An illusion that an object appears larger or smaller by the perceived distance from the viewer.

***Study Tip-* Semantic Encoding**: You can remember information better with personal meaning. Write down examples of the terms from your life or memory. Ex. Flashing Christmas lights make the light seem to move, which is the Phi Phenomenon.

Ames Room	An irregular-shaped room that uses the size-distance relationship to create the illusion of growing and shrinking people.

en:user:Eixo, Ames room, CC BY-SA 3.0

Andrevruas, Casaperspectiva, CC BY 3.0

Müller-Lyer Illusion	• A geometric illusion in which the perceived length of lines varies depending on the direction of connected arrows. • It is likely caused by the learned distance from right angles in rooms.
Poggendorff Illusion	The illusion that two diagonal lines appear offset when they pass behind a vertical barrier.

Perceptual Interpretation	• **Nature v. Nurture** debate of **Perception** • **Immanuel Kant**-knowledge comes from our inborn ways of organizing sensory experience. • **John Locke**- we perceive the world through our experiences.
Sensory Deprivation	Kittens raised without exposure to horizontal lines had difficulty perceiving them.
Restored Vision	• Adults with surgery to correct cataracts • Regained sight • Individuals could distinguish between figure and ground • Could not distinguish shapes

Perceptual Adaptation	<ul><li>The ability of the brain to adjust to changes in visual input</li><li>Goggle experiments- visual input changes to upside down or 30% to the side</li><li>Eventually, the brain adapts, and the person can function normally.</li></ul>

3.5 What are the structures and functions of the parts of the ear?

Outer Ear	
Auditory Canal	Conducts sounds through the external ear.
Pinna	The funnel-shaped part focuses sound toward the auditory canal.
Middle Ear	
Hammer (Malleus), Anvil (Incus), Stirrup (Stapes)	Tiny bones that transmit sound waves to the inner.
Inner Ear	
Cochlea	<ul><li>Snail-like, fluid-filled tube</li><li>Location of acoustical transduction</li></ul>
Semicircular Canals	Location of vestibular sacs. Help with balance.
Vestibular Sacs	Respond to gravity to help determine the head's orientation.
Hair Cells	Sense receptors for hearing

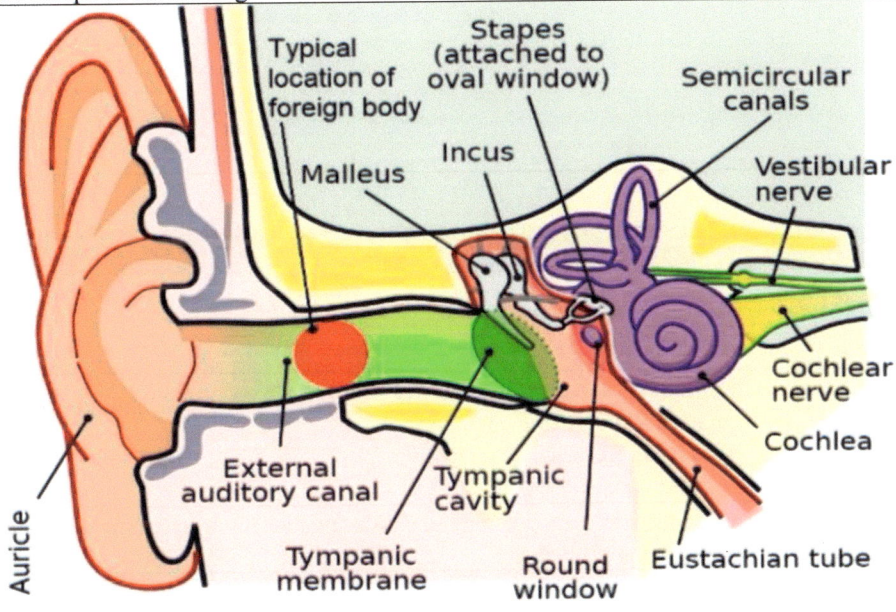

Lars Chittka; Axel Brockmann; James Heilman, EarFB, CC BY-SA 2.5

How do the ears hear?

Acoustical Transduction	Converting sound waves into neural impulses
Sound Waves	Compression and refraction of air molecules
Frequency	<ul><li>Distance from one peak to another.</li><li>Determines pitch</li><li>Short wavelength=high frequency and high-pitched sounds</li><li>Long wavelength=low frequency and low-pitched sounds</li></ul>
Amplitude	<ul><li>Height of the wave</li><li>Determines intensity (perceived loudness)</li></ul>
Decibels	<ul><li>The measure of the intensity of the sound waves</li><li>Decibel measurement increases exponentially. Ex. 10 to 30 decibels increase is 100 times louder. 10 x 10, not 30-10</li></ul>
Timbre	Characteristics of sound

Frequency Theory	• The perception of different pitches is due to the speed of neural impulses. • Some sound wave frequencies are too fast for hair cell firing. • Volley Principle stipulates that hair cells alternate firing for higher frequency waves.
Place Theory	Perception of different pitches is due to the place on the Cochlea that the sound wave stimulates.
Localization of Sound	The brain determines the direction of the sound because it will arrive at one ear before the other.
Conduction Deafness	Loss of hearing due to damage to the eardrum or bones of the middle ear
Sensorineural Hearing Loss	Loss of hearing due to damage to the cochlea, basilar membrane, or hair cells of the inner ear
Cochlear Implants	Electronic devices implanted in the cochlea that electrically stimulate the auditory nerve. 1. external speech processor captures sound and converts it into digital signals 2. processor sends digital signals to internal implant 3. internal implant converts signals into electrical energy, sending it to an electrode array inside the cochlea 4. electrodes stimulate hearing nerve, bypassing damaged hair cells, and the brain perceives signals; you hear sound BC Family Hearing, Cochlear-implant, CC BY-SA 4.0

3.6 How does the sensory system create smell and taste from chemicals?

Olfaction	• Smell • Chemicals received in the nose are transmitted to the olfactory bulb in the brain.
Taste	• Chemicals from food dissolve with saliva and trigger taste receptors on the tongue • Sweet, Sour, Salty, Bitter, Unami (meatiness)
Sensory Interaction	• The integration of multiple senses to perceive • Olfaction greatly influences taste.
Synaesthesia	• A condition when the stimulation of one sense simultaneously triggers the perception of another sense. • Grapheme-Color is the most common. See colors when viewing words and numbers.

3.7 How does the body sense and perceive the world?

Touch	• Specific receptors for warmth, pain, cold, and pressure • Nociceptor- pain • Thermoreceptors- temperature
Phantom Limb	• Pain and sensations felt in a nonexistent limb. • Brain regions receive signals from another location or still fire without sensory input.
Pain	A psychological interpretation of touch.
Gate-Control Theory of Pain	The spinal cord has gates that can open and close in response to pain signals to the brain.
Kinesthesis	Using proprioceptor sensors in muscles, tendons, and joints for position and balance
Vestibular Sense	Using fluid movement in the inner ear's vestibular sacs to maintain balance and equilibrium

Unit 4- Learning (7-9% AP Exam Weighting)

4.1 What is learning?

Learning	Acquiring new behaviors and knowledge
Associative Learning	Acquiring new behaviors and knowledge through connections between elements
Behaviorism	<ul><li>Approach to psychology by John B. Watson.</li><li>Can only objectively study observable behaviors.</li><li>Cannot study qualitative processes such as feelings, thoughts, and motives.</li></ul>

4.2 What is classical conditioning, and how does it work?

Classical Conditioning	<ul><li>Developed by Ivan Pavlov</li><li>Experiments with salivation in dogs</li><li>Type of learning in which one associates a stimulus with an involuntary response.</li></ul>

	Definition	Pavlov's Experiment
Neutral Stimulus (N)	A stimulus that does not trigger a response	The Bell
Unconditioned Stimulus (UCS, US)	<ul><li>A stimulus that causes a UCR</li><li>Not learned</li></ul>	Meat Powder
Unconditioned Response (UCR, UR)	<ul><li>A natural response that occurs without or before any conditioning</li><li>Also called respondent behavior</li></ul>	Salivation
Conditioned Stimulus (CS)	Elicits a response after repeated exposure to a UCS	The Bell
Conditioned Response (CR)	Learned response to a conditioned stimulus	Salivation

The meat powder is only a UCS/US when it is in the mouth of the dog. Seeing the meat powder is not a UCS. They are classically conditioned if the dogs salivate at the sight of meat powder.

Acquisition	Measurable changes in response. An association between a CS and CR.
Extinction	If the CS is not present before the CR, the association lessens, and the CR diminishes.
Spontaneous Recovery	The reappearance of a CR after it was extinct
Generalization	The effects of the conditioning spread beyond the initial N to other similar stimuli.
Discrimination	The ability to distinguish between stimuli and respond differently to them

Taste Aversion	<ul><li>When food is paired with a UCR-usually an illness</li><li>The illness does not have to occur immediately after eating.</li><li>It does not usually require multiple pairings</li><li>Highly resistant to extinction</li></ul>
Higher-Order/Second-Order Conditioning	When the conditioned stimulus acts as an unconditioned stimulus creating a CR to the second UCS

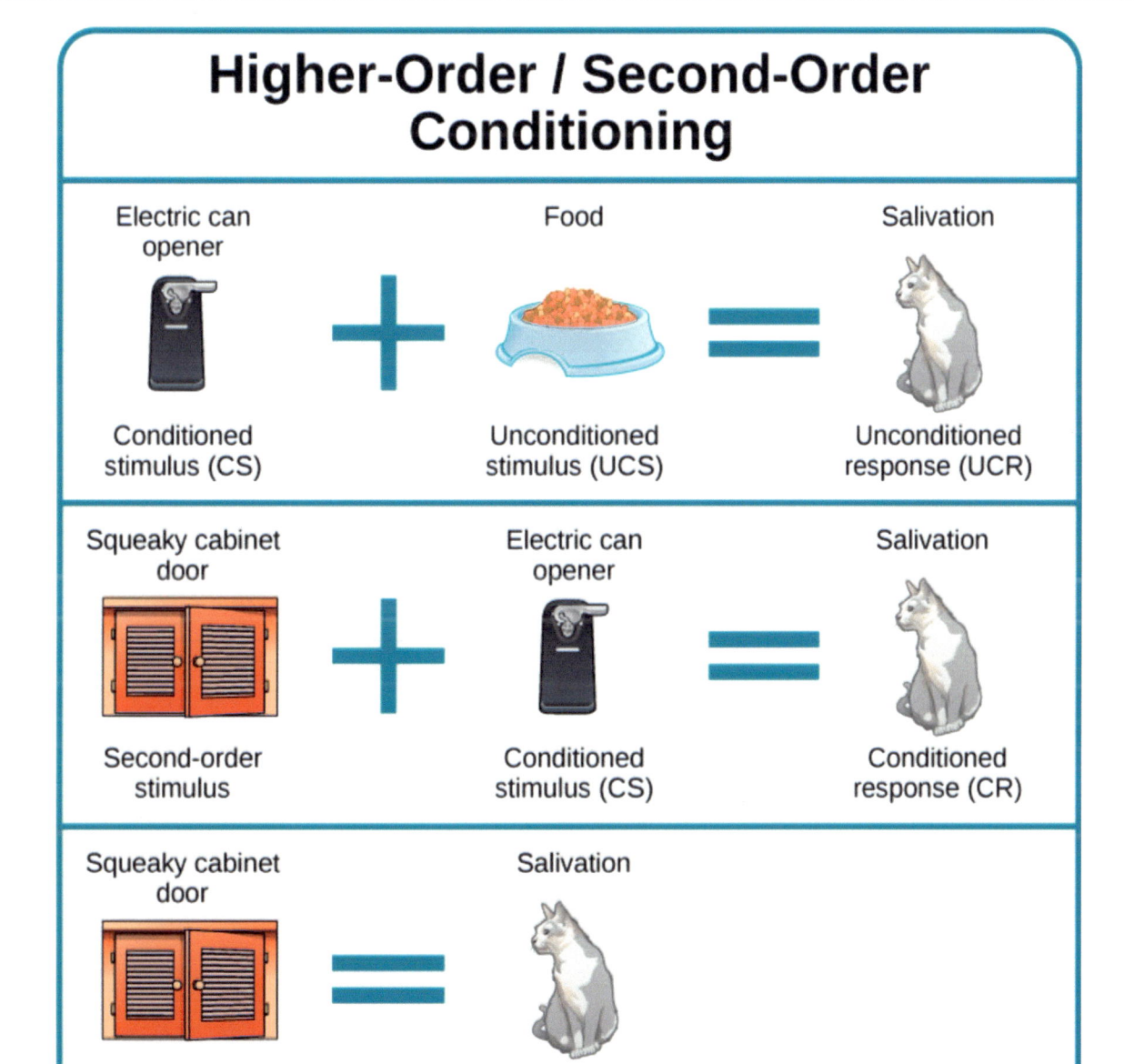

Higher-Order / Second-Order Conditioning

Row 1: Electric can opener (Conditioned stimulus (CS)) + Food (Unconditioned stimulus (UCS)) = Salivation (Unconditioned response (UCR))

Row 2: Squeaky cabinet door (Second-order stimulus) + Electric can opener (Conditioned stimulus (CS)) = Salivation (Conditioned response (CR))

Row 3: Squeaky cabinet door (Second-order stimulus) = Salivation (Conditioned response (CR))

Rose M. Spielman, Ph.D., Second-order conditioning Cat and Can opener and door sound, CC BY 4.0

Baby Albert Experiments by John B. Watson		
Baby Albert	<ul><li>**Classically conditioned** Baby Albert to fear white rats by pairing them with a UCS of a loud noise.</li><li>The fear was generalized to other white furry objects.</li><li>Albert was an orphan</li><li>Watson did not need parental permission</li><li>Unethical by today's guidelines</li><li>Albert was adopted during the experiment and withdrawn from it</li><li>Mystery and investigations surrounding his life outcomes</li></ul>

Order of Presentation

Type	Explanation	Outcome
Delay Conditioning	CS is presented and remains present with a long delay before the UCS	A CR develops
Simultaneous Conditioning	CS and UCS are presented at the same time.	No CR develops
Backward Conditioning	The UCS is presented before the N	No CR develops

4.3 What is operant conditioning, and how does it work?

Operant Conditioning	- First developed by B.F. Skinner - Behavioral change occurs as a response to the consequences of the behavior.
Law of Effect	- First developed by Edward L. Thorndike - The consequences of behavior will change the future probability of the behavior occurring again. - If the behavior produces a satisfying result, one will do the behavior again.

Key distinction- **classical conditioning** requires associating a stimulus with an involuntary behavior, whereas **operant conditioning** is a voluntary behavior followed by a consequence.

What are the types of operant conditioning?

Ask the following two questions to determine the type of operant conditioning:

1) Was something added or subtracted?
2) Was the result/intended result an increase or decrease in behavior?

	Positive- to add something	Negative- to subtract something
Reinforcement- used to increase a behavior	Positive Reinforcement- add something pleasant to increase a behavior.	Negative Reinforcement- subtract something unpleasant to increase a behavior.
Punishment – used to decrease a behavior	Positive Punishment- add something unpleasant to decrease a behavior.	Negative Punishment- subtract something pleasant to decrease a behavior.

Shaping or Shaping by Successive Approximations	- A method of operant conditioning. - Responses roughly approximating the behavior are reinforced. - Later, only behaviors close to the behavior are reinforced. - Eventually, only the behavior is reinforced.

Primary Reinforcers	They increase the chance of a behavior occurring again without needing special experience or knowledge of the stimulus.
Secondary Reinforcers	A previously neutral stimulus acquires the ability to influence the future probability of a behavior because it is associated with a primary reinforcer.
Continuous Reinforcement	Reinforcement every time the behavior occurs
Partial or Intermittent Reinforcement	Only some responses are reinforced.

Ask the following two questions to determine the **schedule of reinforcement:**

1) Was the reinforcement/punishment given in a predicted pattern?
2) Was the reinforcement/punishment provided based on time elapsing?

	Types of Partial Reinforcement		
	Fixed – preset amount	**Variable** - random	
Ratio – the rate of responding	**Fixed-Ratio (FR)-** reinforcement after a fixed number of responses	**Variable-Ratio (VR)-** reinforcement after a random number of responses	
Interval – elapse of time	**Fixed-Interval (FI)-** reinforcement after a fixed period of time elapsed	**Variable-Interval (VI)-** reinforcement after a random amount of time elapsed	

Skinner Box or **Operant Conditioning Chamber**	• An apparatus made by **B.F. Skinner** • Used to test the **schedules of reinforcement** • Blocks out extraneous stimuli • Devices that present stimuli • Typically, a lever that presents food	

Original: AndreasJS Vector: Pixelsquid, Skinner box scheme 01, CC BY-SA 3.0

4.4 What is observational and latent learning, and how do they work?

Observational Learning	• Acquiring new skills, information, or behavior by watching others • **Albert Bandura** • **Bobo Doll Experiment-** children who watched an adult's violent behavior toward the doll, were more likely to imitate the behavior.	

Okhanm, Bobo Doll Deneyi, CC BY-SA 4.0

Modeling	One or more people serve as examples and demonstrate appropriate behavior.
Vicarious Reinforcement	A person becomes more likely to do a behavior because they see other people being reinforced for it.

Cognitive Map	A mental understanding of an environment that actively forms during experiences.
Latent Learning	<ul><li>Learning acquired without conscious effort or reinforcement is only later realized when needed.</li><li>Experiments with rats that randomly explore a maze later navigate them with few errors when a reward is at the end.</li></ul>

Study Tip- **Elaboration/Deep Processing**: Make connections between the terms and other things you are studying in school. Ex. You are reading a book and notice that the main character was **negatively punished** by their parents when they took their cell phone away.

4.5 How do societal and cognitive factors affect learning?

Overjustification Effect	Rewarding a behavior can weaken a performance because the person loses intrinsic motivation.
Prosocial Modeling of Behavior	Modeling behavior that benefits others
Antisocial Modeling of Behavior	Modeling behavior that violates social norms and others' rights

Note- This unit's concepts will help you understand concepts in future units such as **behavior modification, biofeedback, coping strategies, and self-control.**

Unit 5- Cognitive Psychology (13-17 % AP Exam Weighting)

5.1 What are the cognitive processes of memory?

Deep Processing- focusing on meaning instead of characteristics. Creates stronger memory. Often involves relating to other material.

Shallow Processing- focus on characteristics instead of meaning. Creates weaker and shorter-lasting memories.

Cognition	Knowing, perceiving, remembering, reasoning, judging, imagining, and problem-solving
Metacognition	Thinking about one's thinking. Often with an attempt to exercise conscious control
Concept	An idea that represents a grouping of objects by their essential properties
Prototype	The best or average exemplar of a concept

What is the memory process?

Information-Processing Model	• Compares human memory to a computer • It involves encoding, storage, and retrieval	
	Encoding	The process of getting information into the memory system
	Storage	The process of retaining information over time
	Retrieval	The process of getting information out of memory storage

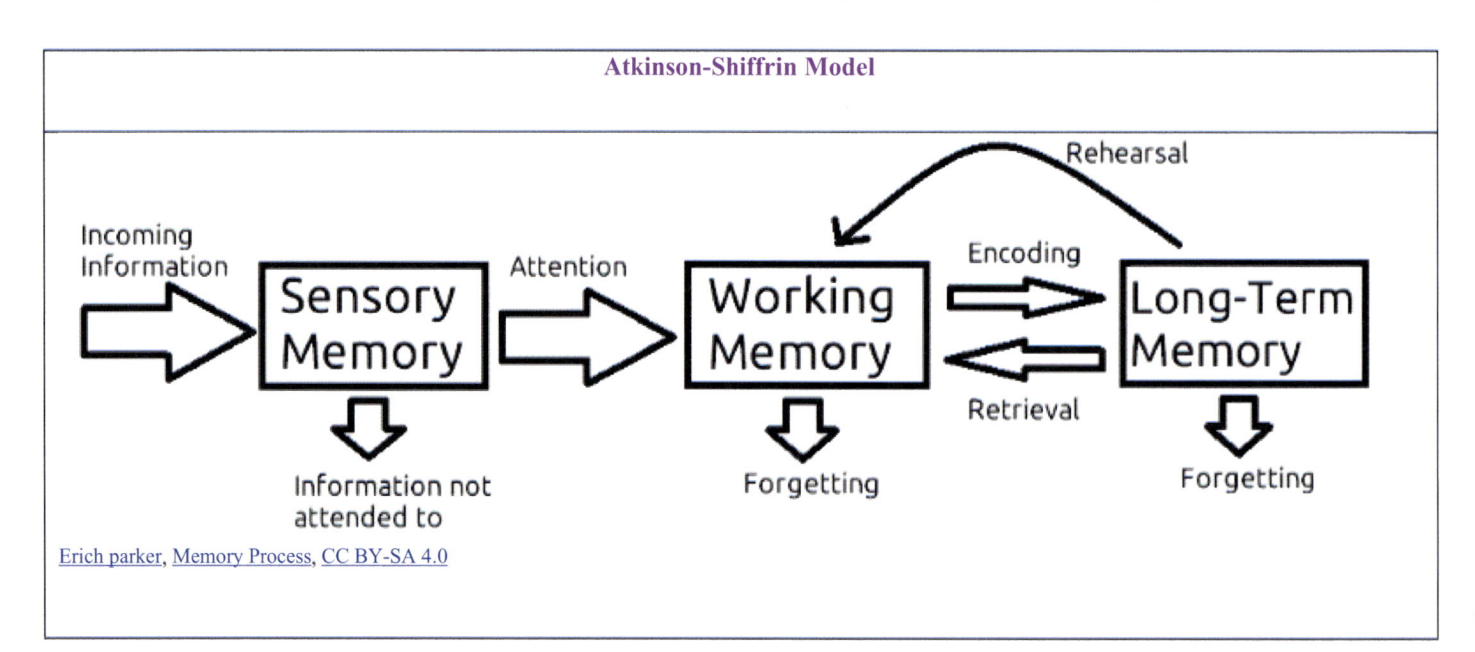

Atkinson-Shiffrin Model

Incoming Information → Sensory Memory → (Attention) → Working Memory ⇄ Long-Term Memory

Rehearsal (from Long-Term Memory back to Working Memory)
Encoding (Working Memory to Long-Term Memory)
Retrieval (Long-Term Memory to Working Memory)

Sensory Memory → Information not attended to
Working Memory → Forgetting
Long-Term Memory → Forgetting

Erich parker, Memory Process, CC BY-SA 4.0

Sensory Memory	Brief storage of sensory information.
George Sperling	Experiments with sensory memory. Flashed letters for a millisecond to participants. It demonstrated that the letters were in sensory memory but quickly forgotten.

Iconic Memory	Type of sensory memory that is for visual stimuli. Sperling demonstrated that it lasts less than a second.
Echoic Memory	Type of sensory memory that is for auditory stimuli. Sperling demonstrated that it lasts 3-4 seconds.
Hepatic Memory	Type of sensory memory that is for touch stimuli. Sperling demonstrated that it lasts about 1 second.

Short-Term Memory (STM)	• The reproduction, recall, or recognition of information for 10-30 seconds after someone presents it. • George Miller- 7 +/- 2 digits

Working Memory (WM)	• **Alan Baddeley** • States that STM is too simple. • WM includes visual and auditory rehearsal • A central executive that focuses attention • The central executive pulls relevant information from long-term memory	
	Visuospatial Sketchpad	Part of WM that briefly holds the appearance of objects and their location in space.
	Phonological Loop	Part of WM that briefly holds and manipulates auditory information.
	Episodic Buffer	Combines information from the visuospatial sketchpad and phonological loop with information about time to create an integrated episode.
	Central Executive	• Part of WM that manages the visuospatial sketchpad, phonological loop, and accesses relevant information from long-term memory. • It focuses attention and switches between tasks.

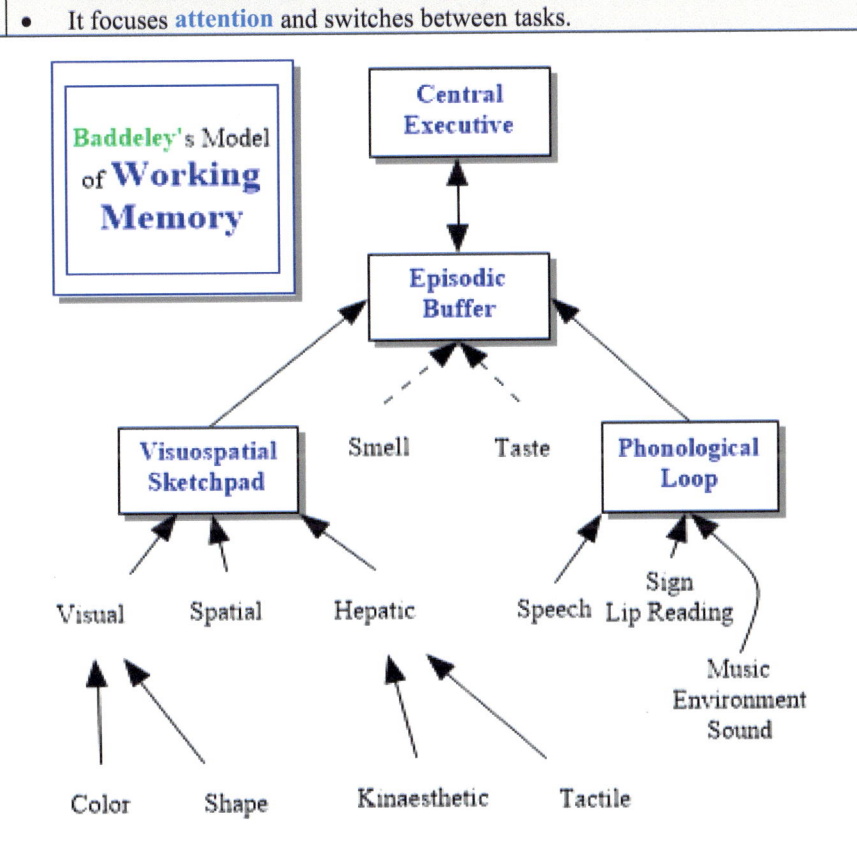

Baddeley's Model of Working Memory diagram: Central Executive ↔ Episodic Buffer, which receives inputs from Visuospatial Sketchpad (Visual, Spatial, Hepatic → Color, Shape, Kinaesthetic, Tactile), Smell, Taste, and Phonological Loop (Speech, Sign Lip Reading, Music, Environment Sound).

Long-Term Memory (LTM)	A relatively permanent storage system of knowledge and skills that can last for hours, weeks, and years	
	Declarative Memory	• Type of LTM • Events or facts • Two types: Episodic and Semantic
	Episodic Memory	A memory of personally experienced events
	Semantic Memory	General knowledge, facts, concepts
	Procedural Memory	• Type of LTM • How to perform skills physically
	Rehearsal	Repetition increases long-term storage.

5.2 What is encoding, and how does it work?

Acoustic Encoding	The process of taking in sound and converting it into a mental representation that can be stored
Visual Encoding	The process of taking in light and converting it into a mental representation that can be stored
Semantic Encoding	<ul><li>The process of taking in stimuli and focusing on the meaning of it instead of the perceptual aspects</li><li>Often involves **elaboration**</li><li>**Craig and Tulving-** experiments demonstrated that participants remembered semantically encoded material better than acoustic and visual.</li></ul>
Elaboration	<ul><li>Linking information with other material.</li></ul>

Selective Attention- concentrating on only certain stimuli in an environment while ignoring others.

Divided Attention- concentrating on two or more sources of information at the same time.

5.3 What are the principles for the effective storage of memories?

Effortful Processing Strategies	
Chunking	<ul><li>The process of dividing large pieces of information into pieces or "chunks."</li><li>**Short-term memory can** hold 7 +/- 2 pieces of information. It can also hold seven chunks, increasing its capacity.</li></ul>
Mnemonic	A device used to assist memory.
Peg-Word System	<ul><li>A **mnemonic device** that associates each item with a peg</li><li>One is a bun, two is a shoe, etc.</li><li>Associating each item with the peg word increases the ability to remember.</li></ul>
Key-Word Method	A **mnemonic device** that associates the sound of the word with another mental image
Method of Loci	A **mnemonic device** that associates each item with a mental image of a specific location

Study Tip- **Method of Loci:** Take each term and place it in a location in your house. Ex. Visualize that there are gummy bears stuck together on the floor of your kitchen because chunking is putting information together to memorize it. Then visualize that you used M&Ms instead of coffee grounds in your coffee pot because Mnemonics are memory devices. Do this same thing for each term on the list, and then all you will have to do to remember them all is visually take a walk through your house.

More Effortful Processing Strategies	
Hierarchical Organization	Organizing information in categories and subcategories
Spacing Effect	Information learned in short study sessions with gaps in-between restudying is better remembered than massed practice.
Distributed Practice	Space out practice periods for a task with lengthy rest in between, resulting in better memory of the material.
Massed Practice	Practice periods are close together or all at once. Not as effective as distributed practice.
Testing Effect	The research finding that taking a test leads to better retention than restudying the material for the same time

5.4 What are the principles of retrieval of memories?

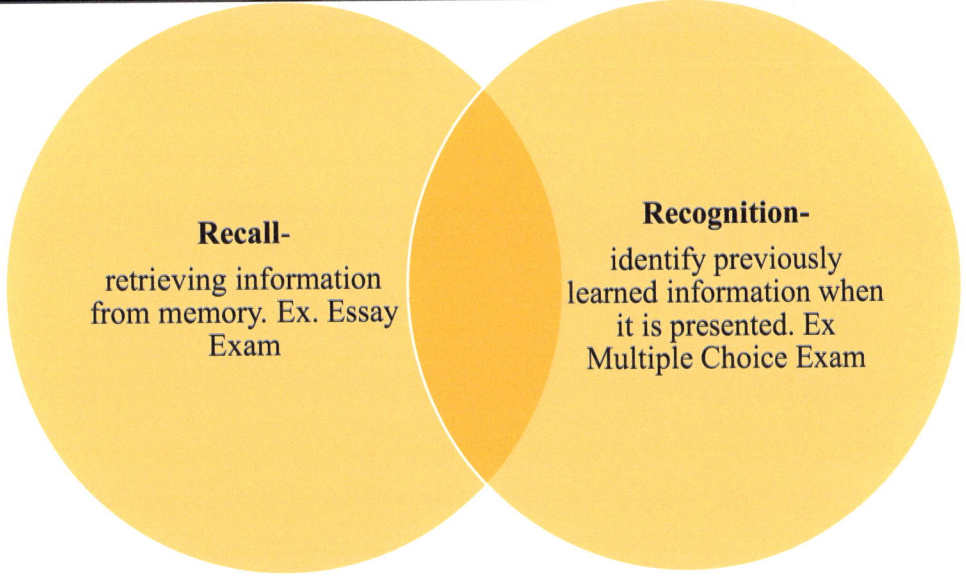

Recall- retrieving information from memory. Ex. Essay Exam

Recognition- identify previously learned information when it is presented. Ex Multiple Choice Exam

Retrieval Cues	<ul><li>People hold memories in a web of associations.</li><li>Retrieval cues are pathways or triggers to activate the memory.</li><li>Primary- directly related,</li><li>Secondary- related to an item that is related to the item</li><li>Tertiary- more than two away, but still activates the memory.</li></ul>
Priming	A stimulus that acts as a retrieval cue
Context-Dependent Memory	Improved recall when the context present at encoding and retrieval are the same. Ex. Same room.
State-Dependent Memory	Improved recall when the same biological or psychological state is present at encoding and retrieval. Ex. alcohol
Mood-Congruent Memory	Improved recall when the same mood is present at encoding and retrieval. Ex. happy

Serial Positioning Effect	People remember items at the beginning and end better.
Primacy Effect	People remember the first item better than the material later in the sequence.
Recency	People remember the most recently presented items better than those in the middle.

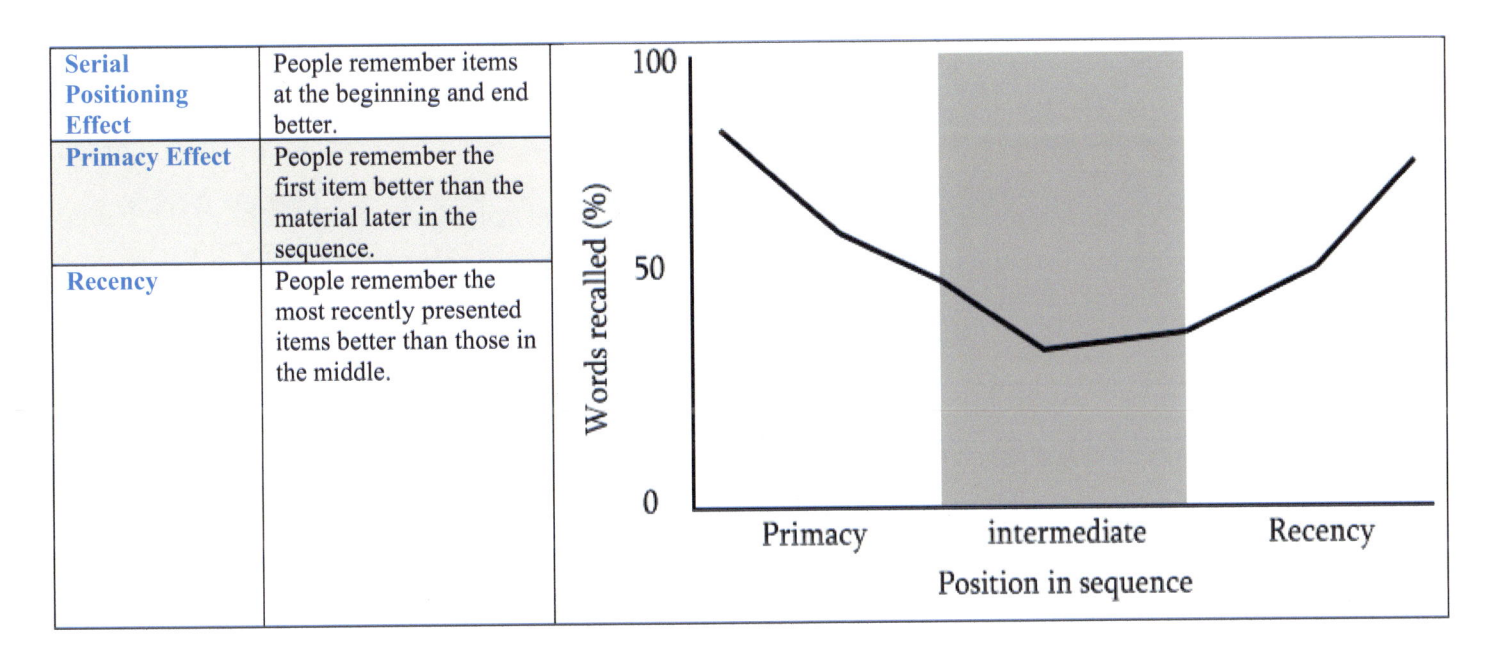

***Study Tip-* Serial Position Effect**: Practice recalling the most challenging material at the beginning and end of your study session.

5.5 What are memory errors, and why are they committed?

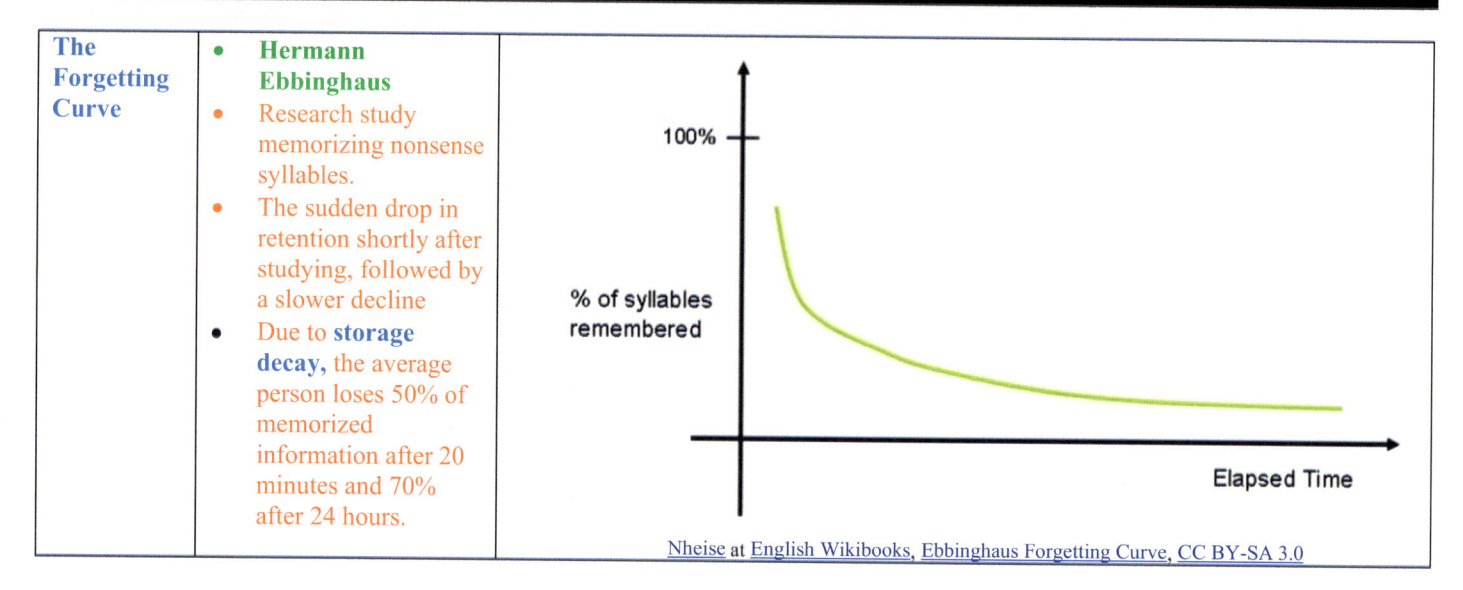

The Forgetting Curve	<ul><li>**Hermann Ebbinghaus**</li><li>Research study memorizing nonsense syllables.</li><li>The sudden drop in retention shortly after studying, followed by a slower decline</li><li>Due to **storage decay,** the average person loses 50% of memorized information after 20 minutes and 70% after 24 hours.</li></ul>	*Graph: Ebbinghaus Forgetting Curve showing % of syllables remembered (y-axis, 100%) vs Elapsed Time (x-axis), with a rapidly declining curve.* Nheise at English Wikibooks, Ebbinghaus Forgetting Curve, CC BY-SA 3.0

Encoding Failure or Absentmindedness	Failure to notice or encode information.
Storage Decay or Transience	<ul><li>Memorized material fades over time</li><li>The **forgetting curve.**</li></ul>
Tip-of-the-Tongue or Blocking	The experience of trying to retrieve something from memory unsuccessfully

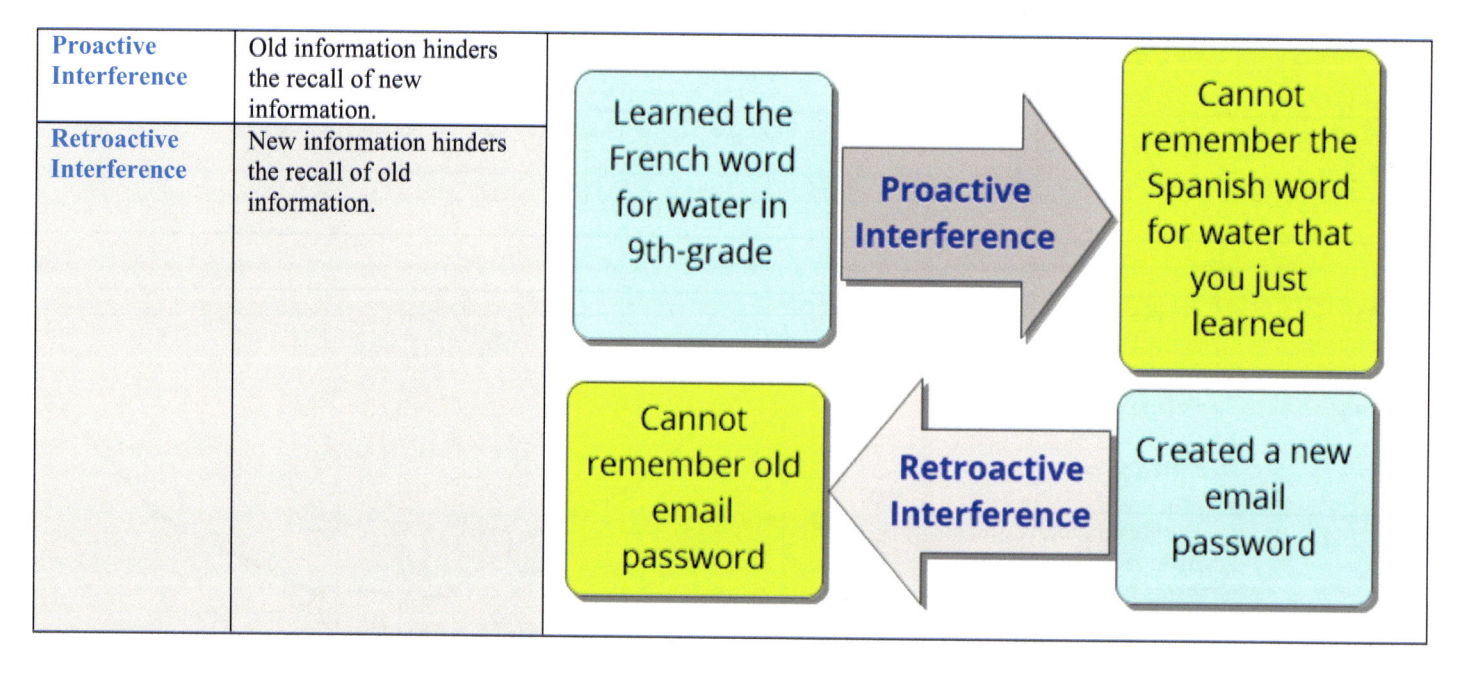

Proactive Interference	Old information hinders the recall of new information.	*Diagram: Learned the French word for water in 9th-grade → Proactive Interference → Cannot remember the Spanish word for water that you just learned. Created a new email password → Retroactive Interference → Cannot remember old email password.*
Retroactive Interference	New information hinders the recall of old information.	

Motivated Forgetting	A desire to avoid a painful memory
Misinformation Effect or Suggestibility	<ul><li>Researchers study it in connection with eyewitness testimony.</li><li>Recall misleading information that someone (researcher, lawyer) provided instead of the correct information.</li><li>**Elizabeth Loftus**</li></ul>
Imagination Effect	Repeatedly imagining fake events or actions creates false memories.
Source Amnesia or Source Misattribution	Confusion about the information's source (how, when, where)
Déjà Vu	The feeling of experiencing an event before

5.6 What are the biological bases of memory?

Long-Term Potentiation	- **Neural** change - **Neurons** that fire together, wire together. - Increased sensitivity at the **synapse** - **Kandel** - **Aplysia-** sea slug studies
Memory Consolidation	Neurobiological change following a learning experience. Transfer to **long-term memory.**
Flashbulb Memory	- A personally significant and emotional events often have the quality of a photograph. - The accuracy of flashbulb memories decreases with time. - The release of **epinephrine** helps create instant **long-term memory,** according to the **James McGaugh** rat study.

Hippocampus	- **Declarative memories** - Processes **explicit memories**, doesn't store - **Spatial memory**
Cerebellum	- **Implicit memories** such as motor **learning** and **classical conditioning**
Amygdala	- It is involved in **memory consolidation**. - Emotions help memory

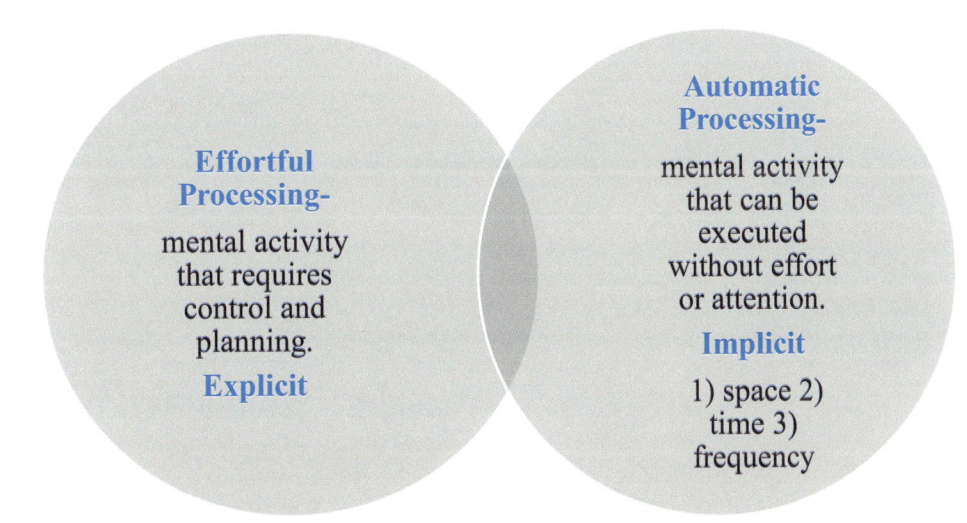

Effortful Processing- mental activity that requires control and planning. **Explicit**

Automatic Processing- mental activity that can be executed without effort or attention. **Implicit**
1) space 2) time 3) frequency

5.7 What are the methods to solve problems?

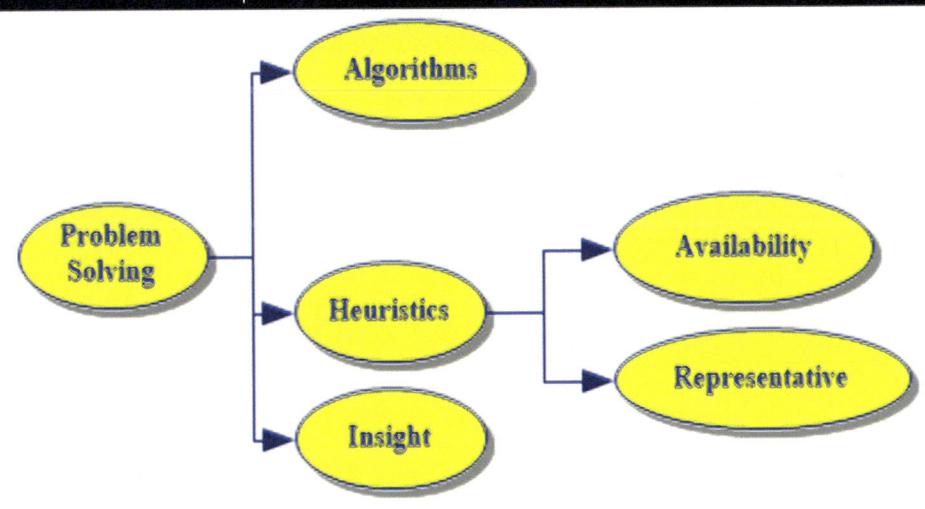

Problem Solving
- Algorithms
- Heuristics
  - Availability
  - Representative
- Insight

Strategy	Description	Strengths and Weaknesses
Insight	<ul><li>The sudden solution to a problem by means that are not usually obvious</li><li>It just pops into one's head.</li><li>Wolfgang Köhler – studied the mentality of apes when problem-solving.</li></ul>	<ul><li>Fast</li><li>It does not always result in a solution</li></ul>
Algorithm	A set procedure for solving a problem that often involves a series of steps that eliminate possible combinations	<ul><li>Accurate</li><li>Time-consuming</li></ul>
Availability Heuristic	<ul><li>Judging based on the relevant information in memory</li><li>Kahneman and Tversky</li></ul>	<ul><li>Fast</li><li>Inaccurate when information in memory leads one to believe something is more/less common than it is.</li></ul>
Representative Heuristic	<ul><li>Judging based on how much resemblance there is to a typical or average member of the category</li><li>Kahneman and Tversky</li></ul>	<ul><li>Fast</li><li>It can be inaccurate when someone gives too much/too little weight to the rate of occurrence</li></ul>

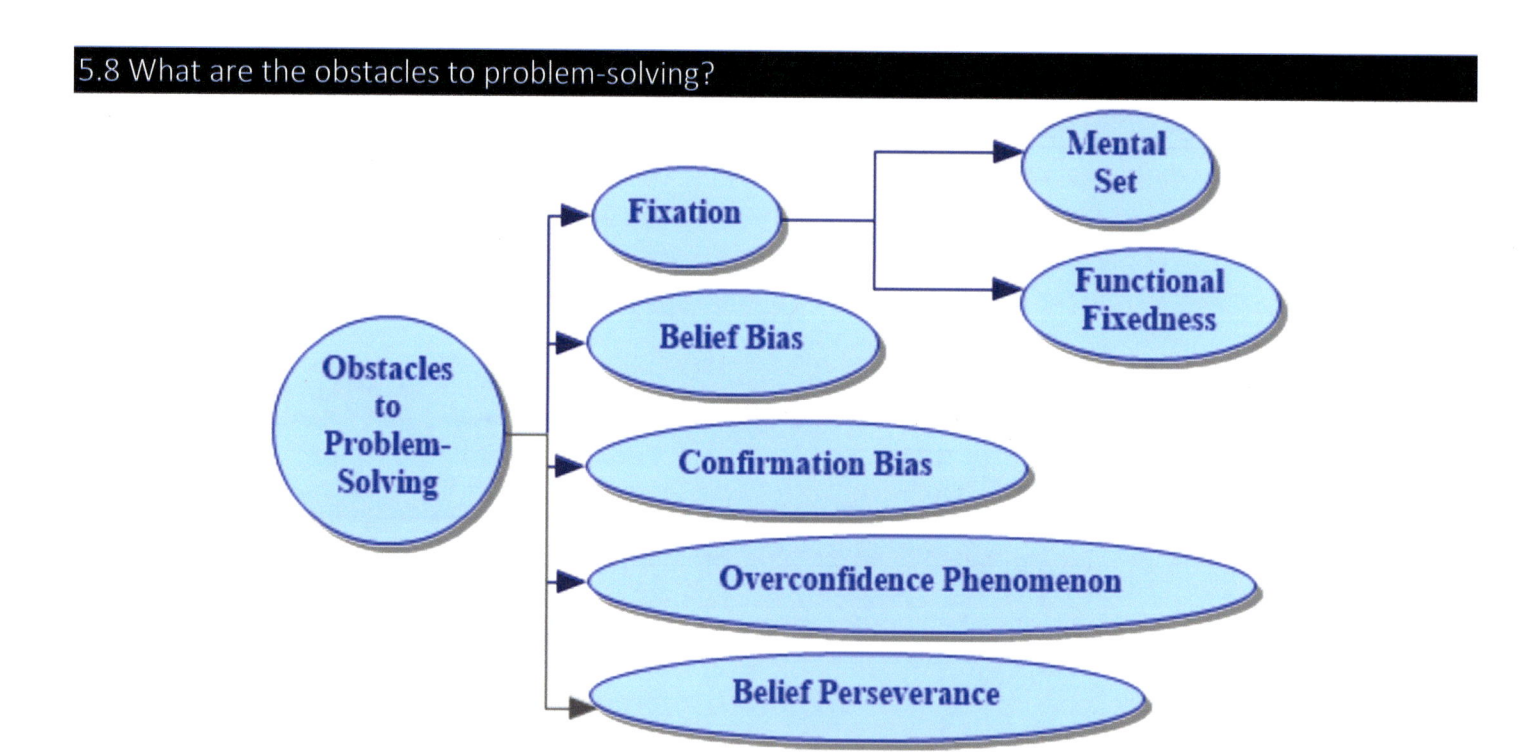

5.8 What are the obstacles to problem-solving?

Obstacles to Problem-Solving:
- Fixation
  - Mental Set
  - Functional Fixedness
- Belief Bias
- Confirmation Bias
- Overconfidence Phenomenon
- Belief Perseverance

Fixation	Focusing on a single idea makes it difficult to examine the problem from another perspective.
Mental Set	The readiness to perform a task or solve a problem based on previously successful techniques or experiences
Functional Fixedness	Perceiving an object only based on its most common use
Belief Bias	Relying on personal knowledge and beliefs to accept conclusions as valid even in the face of conflicting evidence
Confirmation Bias	Gather evidence supporting a conclusion while ignoring or not seeking evidence that refutes it.
Overconfidence Phenomenon	A cognitive bias and overestimation of one's ability to perform a task successfully
Belief Perseverance	Continual belief in an idea even after it was refuted or proven inaccurate

5.9 What is intelligence?

Intelligence	The ability to learn, adapt, understand, think, and reason.

What are the theories of intelligence?

Theory	Person	Idea
Growth Mindset	Carol Dweck	Intelligence is changeable with increased effort instead of ability. Resiliency
Emotional Intelligence	Mayer and Salovey	1. Perceive and appraise emotions 2. Access and evoke emotions for cognition 3. Comprehend emotional language 4. Regulate own and others' emotions for growth
Theory	**Person**	**Idea**
General Intelligence (G)	Charles Spearman	A general intelligence (g factor) supports all other abilities.
Triarchic Theory of Intelligence	Robert J. Sternberg	Three key abilities: analytical, creative, and practical
Multiple Intelligences	Howard Gardner	Eight/nine separate intelligences. Existential?

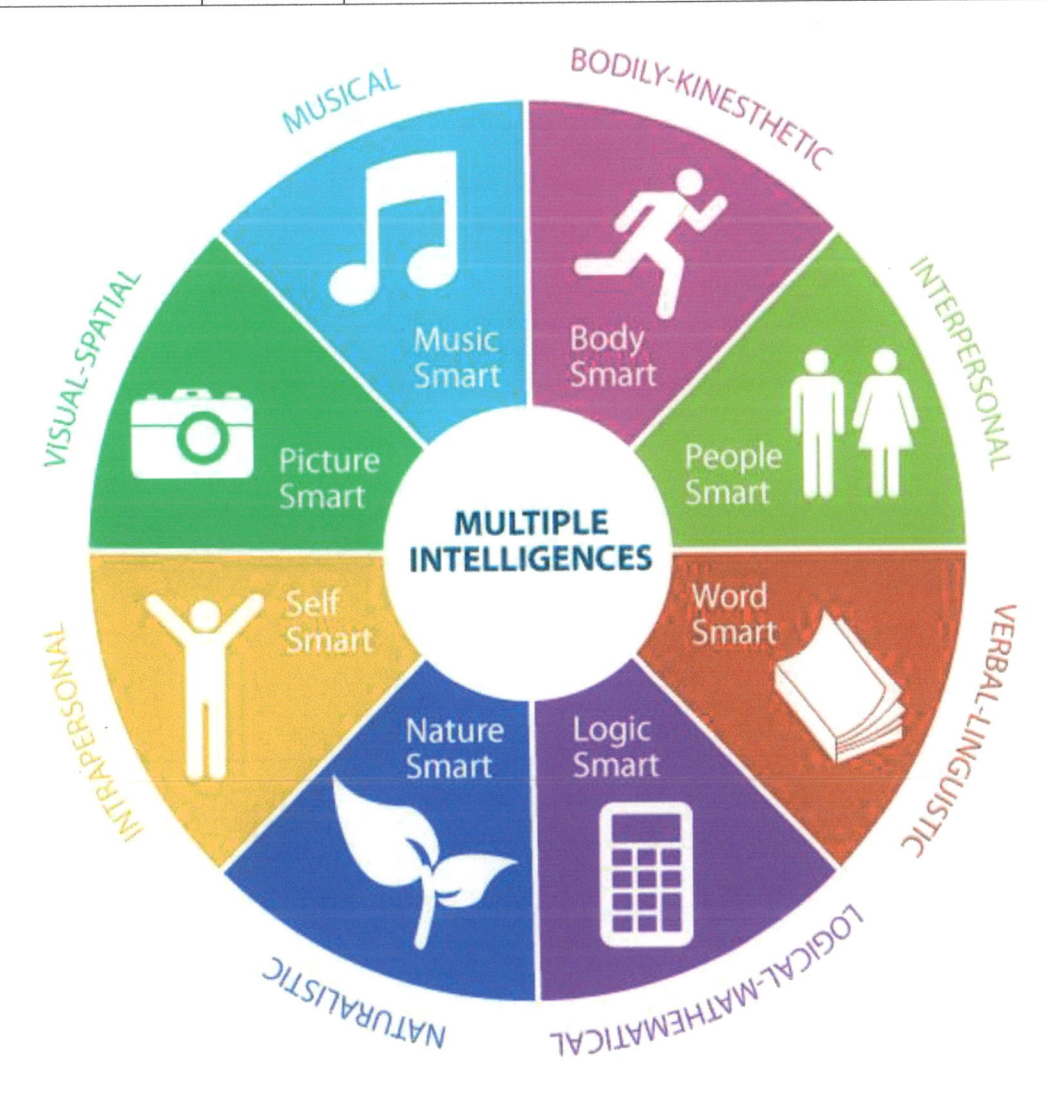

Sajaganesandip, Multiple-intelligence, CC BY-SA 4.0

Fluid Intelligence
Dealing with novel tasks.

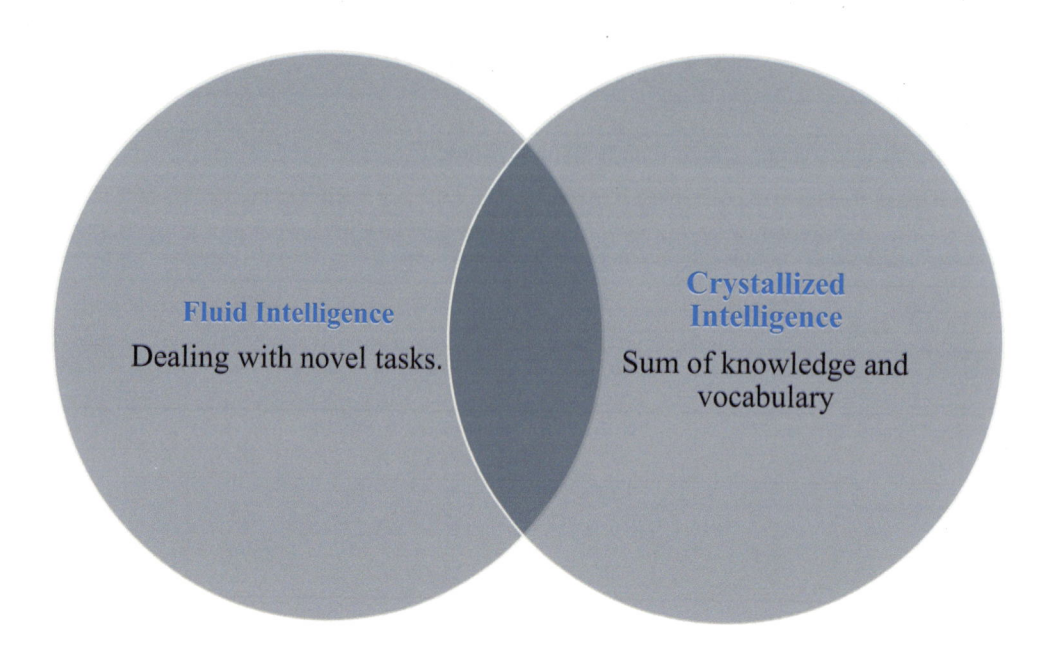

Crystallized Intelligence
Sum of knowledge and vocabulary

5.11 How have psychologists measured intelligence throughout its history?

Francis Galton	- Wanted to quantify human superiority. - **Eugenics** movement.
Eugenics	- Based on **Darwin's** theory of evolution - Selective breeding to improve the population
Alfred Binet	- Founder of modern intelligence testing. - Identify students who would have trouble in classrooms. - Provided a **mental age**
Mental Age	- Performance measure of someone typical for that age
Lewis Terman	- He developed the current **Stanford-Binet Intelligence test** widely used. - Used for army recruits - Used to identify his **Termites**- high IQ students - IQ =mental age/chronological age x 100 - Nobody uses this formula anymore

Wechsler Intelligence Scale for Children (WISC), Wechsler Adult Intelligence Scale (WAIS)	- One of the most commonly utilized intelligence tests - Eleven subtests with separate scores in each category in addition to the overall score - It can help in school to identify learning differences.
Intelligence Quotient (IQ)	- Unfixed - Not a "thing." - A measure of intelligence based on a score on a test - **Standardized** – see a bell curve. Identify the **mean score** and **standard deviation** for each age.
Reification	Viewing abstract immaterial concepts as if they were a thing.

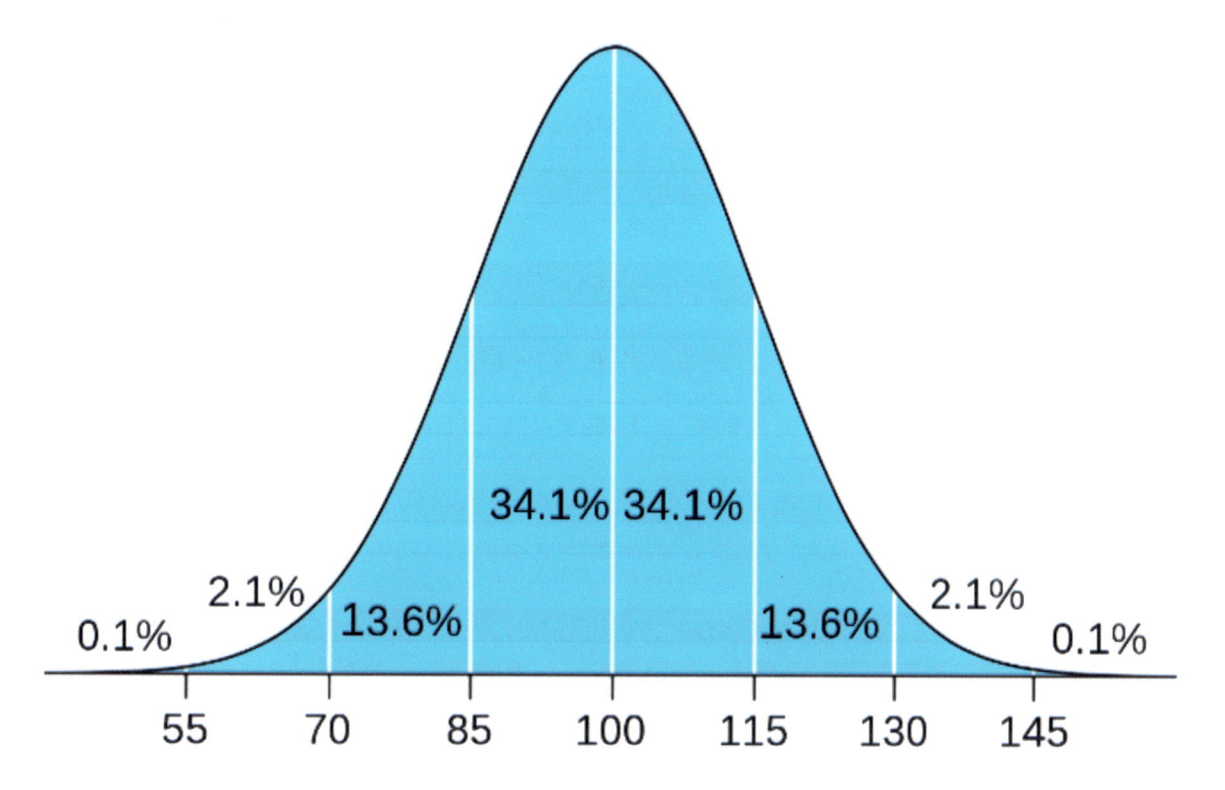

Dmcq, IQ distribution, CC BY-SA 3.0

Important IQ Markers		
70 and Below	100	130 and Above
Intellectual Disability	Mean and Median	Gifted

Savant Syndrome	An **intellectual disability** with exceptional cognitive ability in one area, such as rapid mathematical calculation
Flynn Effect	The gradual increase in **IQ** each generation (30 years)
Stereotype Threat	An individual's expectation of negative stereotypes adversely affects performance on intelligence tests.

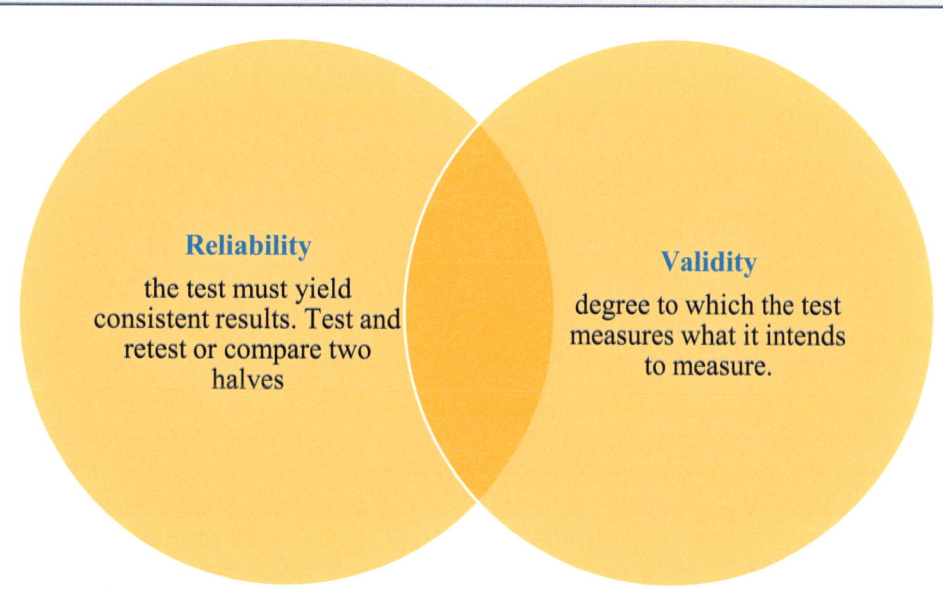

Reliability
the test must yield consistent results. Test and retest or compare two halves

Validity
degree to which the test measures what it intends to measure.

Content Validity	The extent to which the test measures a **representative sample** of the subject matter.
Predictive Validity/Criterion-Related Validity	The extent to which the test **correlates** with a variable in the future.

What are the other types of tests?

Aptitude Test	An assessment designed to measure potential.
Achievement Test	An assessment designed to measure current levels of skill or knowledge in a given subject.
Divergent Test	Test of creativity that scores for the ability deviate from common.

5.12 How is language produced?

Language	A communication system using spoken, written, and/or gestured symbols creates meaning.
Phonemes	The smallest sound of a spoken language
Morphemes	The smallest unit of language that carries meaning

Syntax	A set of rules that explain how people should arrange words and phrases into grammatical sentences
Semantics	Component of language that deals with the meaning

What are the stages of language development?

Stage	Age	Development
Babbling	4 months	Makes sounds, but not always in the language of the household
Babbling	Ten months	Makes sounds of the languages spoken around them
One-Word Stage	1-2 years-old	Speak single words
Two-Word Stage	2-years-old	Speak in two-word phrases that resemble telegraphic speech

Receptive Language	The language that is perceived and mentally processed. It begins around four months
Production Language	Ability to make words
Critical Period	An early stage in life when one is open to learning a language

How is language acquired, and what are its purposes?

Language Acquisition Device	<ul><li>Initially proposed by Benjamin Lee Whorf and later updated by Noam Chomsky.</li><li>An inherited mechanism and innate knowledge that allows for language development and interpretation of the input</li><li>Chomsky added the idea of universal grammar.</li></ul>
Universal Grammar	<ul><li>Languages share basic elements</li><li>Humans are born with the predisposition to learn grammar rules.</li></ul>
Sapir-Whorf Hypothesis or Linguistic Determinism	<ul><li>Edward Sapir and Benjamin Lee Whorf</li><li>Language determines thinking</li><li>Languages differ in how they refer to items such as space, time, duration, and other basic categories.</li></ul>

Unit 6- Developmental Psychology (7-9% AP Exam Weighting)

6.1 What are the factors of prenatal and childhood physical development?

Nature
The genetically inherited characteristics and behaviors of an individual.

Nurture
The environmental factors that influence behavior.

Prenatal Development	
Conception	A sperm cell (male) penetrates the outer coating of an egg (female) and fuses to form one cell.
Zygotes	• Fertilized eggs • Less than half survive longer than two weeks
Embryo	First two months of pregnancy
Fetus	Two months until the end of pregnancy
Placenta	Produced by the embryo and attaches to the uterus wall to function as a provider of nutrients and remove waste products.
Teratogens	An agent that produces abnormalities in a fetus
Fetal Alcohol Syndrome	Heavy maternal alcohol intake causes developmental problems such as low birth weight, neurobehavioral, cognitive deficits, and intellectual disabilities

9 weeks — Fetal stage begins
12 weeks — Sex organs differentiate
16 weeks — Fingers and toes develop
20 weeks — Hearing begins
24 weeks — Lungs begin to develop
28 weeks — Brain grows rapidly
32 weeks — Bones fully develop
36 weeks — Muscles fully develop
40 weeks — Full-term development

https://iastate.pressbooks.pub/parentingfamilydiversity/chapter/prenatal-development/

X Chromosome	• Determines femaleness in humans. • Women (XX) • Male (XY) • Carries around 2000 genes
Y Chromosome	Determines the maleness in humans and other mammals

Infancy and Childhood Physical Development	
Infancy	The earliest period of postnatal life, from birth to about one-year-old
Rooting Reflex	• Automatic and unlearned response of a newborn • They turn in suck in the direction of a stimulus applied to the cheek or corner of the mouth.
Maturation	Naturally occurring time-related changes
Developmental Milestones	• Any physical, cognitive, social, or emotional change that is predictable throughout the world • Ex. Learning to walk around the age of 1.

Stebanoid, Kamensky First Step, CC BY-SA 3.0

6.2 What are the social factors of development?

Temperament	Biologically determined aspects of personality such as energy level, demeanor, mood, and emotional responsiveness. Shy-bold continuum.
Socialization	The process of acquiring social skills, societal beliefs, family values, and behaviors needs to function in society.
Imprinting	Learning process during the critical period when some animals follow the first moving object they see.
Attachment	The emotional bond between an infant and its parent, caregiver, or nonhuman animal provides a feeling of security and calm. **John Bowlby**

***Study Tip-* Chunking and Semantic Encoding**: Study terms in organized groups. I organized this study guide with related terms grouped in tables. See if you can determine the reason for the groupings (semantic encoding). Then, study a table by covering the definitions and attempting to retrieve their definitions or meanings. Once you master a table, move to a new one and repeat.

Harlow's Monkey Studies	• **Harry and Margaret Harlow** • They placed baby monkeys in cages with two fake mother monkeys: One with a cheesecloth baby blanket and the other with only the wires and bottle for feeding. • Baby monkeys spent most of their time on the cloth mother. • The monkeys ran to the cloth mother when experiencing fear-inducing situations. • Conclusion- body contact is more important than nourishment.

| Secure Attachment | • Positive parent-child relationship
• Confidence when the parent is present.
• Explores and uses the parent as a secure base.
• Shows mild distress when the parent leaves.
• The infant goes to the parent when they return |
|---|---|
| Insecure Attachment | • Negative parent-child relationship
• Clings to parent (anxious) or ignores parent presence (ambivalent)
• Shows extreme distress (anxious) or no distress (ambivalent) when the parent leaves.
• Reacts with avoidance or ambivalence upon their return |
Disruption of Attachment	Moving from one caretaker to another. Ex. Foster children
Deprivation of Attachment	Neglect during the critical period. Causes withdrawal, fear and worse in extreme cases
Stranger Anxiety	Distress around unfamiliar individuals usually begins around 8 to 9 months and lasts until age 2.

| Strange Situation | • Mary Ainsworth
• An experiment used to assess the quality of attachment
• A stranger enters the room, and the parent leaves twice.
• Tests secure versus insecure attachment. |
|---|---|

What are the influences of parents on a child's social development?

Diana Baumrind's Parenting Styles- Parents' interactions with children on dimensions of emotionally warm vs. cold and high control vs. low control.	
Authoritarian	Stresses obedience, little to no collaboration, strong punishment
Permissive	Makes few demands and avoids exercising control and punishment
Authoritative	Encourages autonomy but still places limitations. Discusses punishments and reasons for discipline and allows exceptions
Rejecting-Neglecting	Unsupportive and fails to monitor. Attends to own needs above the child

6.3 How do cognitive abilities change throughout life?

Infantile Amnesia	The inability to remember events from early childhood because cognitive abilities for encoding long-term memory have not yet developed, and/or the brain areas for remembering have not yet matured.
Neural Plasticity or Neuroplasticity	The ability of the nervous system to change to environmental stimuli. Neurons rewire based on changes
Pruning	The brain eliminates excessive or redundant neurons and synaptic connections at puberty's onset.

Schema	Basic knowledge about a concept that serves as a guide

Child learns the word "dog" → Dog → Develops a **schema** for dogs → Dogs have four legs

Assimilate	**Jean Piaget-** The process of incorporating new information into preexisting schema based on similarities.	*Schema Assimilation diagram: Child learns the word "dog" → Develops a schema for dogs (Dogs have four legs) → Child sees a horse and calls it a "dog" → The child assimilates the new information into their schema for dogs (Dogs have four legs, they are large, and have manes).*
Accommodate	**Jean Piaget-** Already existing schema changed to incorporate new information.	*Schema Accommodation diagram: Child says "Look Mom, a dog." Mom replies "That is not a dog, it is a horse." The child accommodates the new information into their schema for dogs and a new schema for horses (Dogs have four legs, but do not have manes; Horses have four legs, are large, and have manes).*

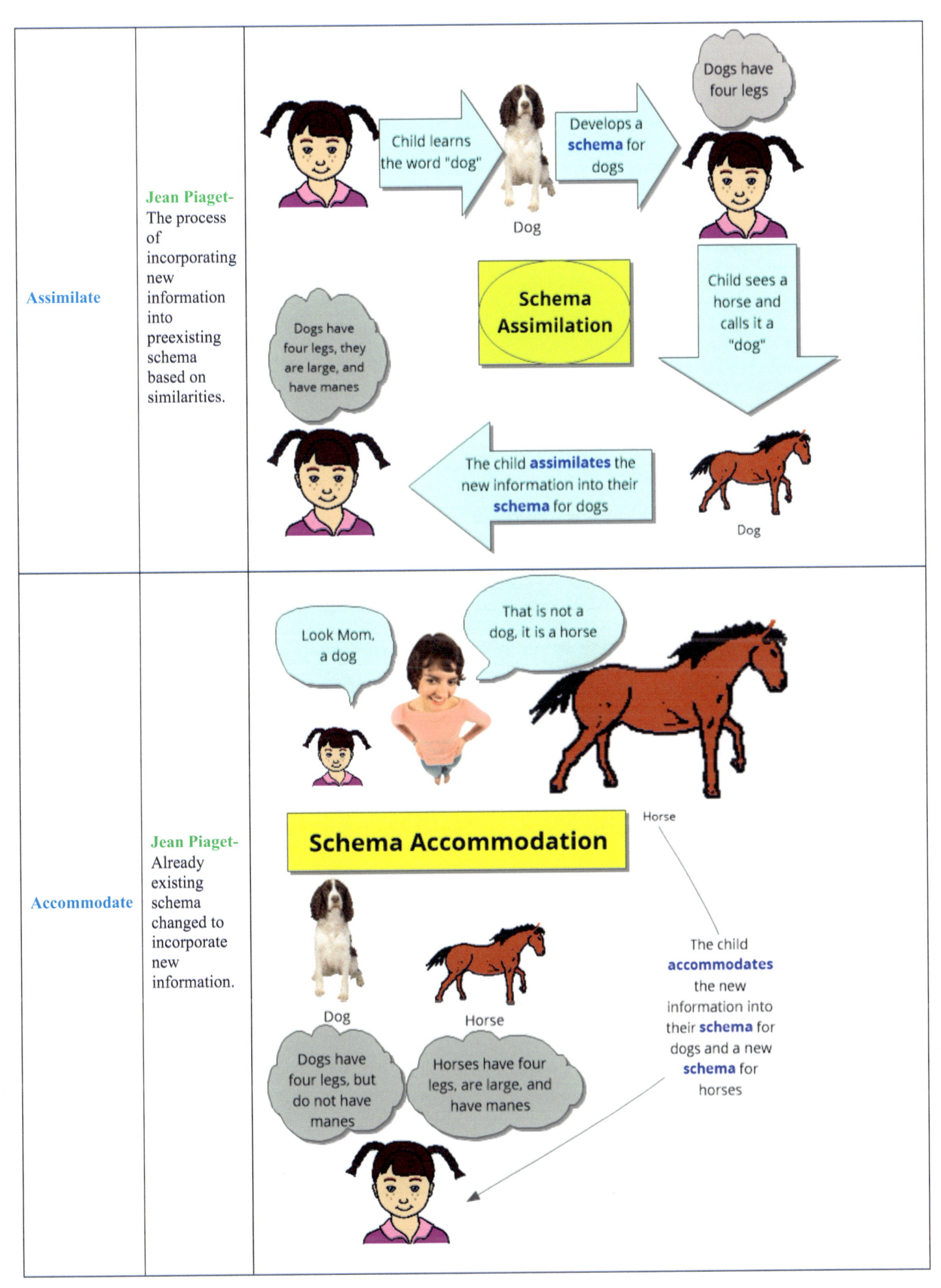

52

Piaget's Stages of Cognitive Development

Age Range	Name of the Stage and Description	Phenomena
Birth to 2-years	**Sensorimotor-** newborn capabilities of basic reflexes such as sucking to more complex repetitive behavior	- Object Permanence - Stranger Anxiety
2-6	**Preoperational-** child shows little awareness of the perspective of others, language and number systems develop, and they can use symbols for expression.	- Pretend Play - Egocentrism - Language
7-11	**Concrete Operational-** more logical and conceptual thinking with a move away from egocentric thinking	- Conservation - Mathematical Transformations
12-Adulthood	**Formal Operational-** abstract logical and moral reasoning	- Abstract Logic

Piagetian Developmental Phenomena

Object Permanence	The ability to understand that objects continue to exist even when not perceived
Pretend Play	Make-believe fantasy play where children take the roles of those known to them, such as mother, father, doctor, etc
Egocentrism	Believing that others see, feel, and understand things from the same point of view as oneself.
Theory of Mind	The understanding that others have different thoughts, beliefs, and emotions than one's own.
Conservation	The understanding that something does not change even when its physical appearance changes.

Lev Vygotsky's Theory of Cognitive Development

Sociocultural Theory	Children observe their environment, culture, and native languages and make them part of themselves.
Internalization	Assimilating parts of a culture such as beliefs, feelings, and attitudes into one's sense of self
Zone of Proximal Development	The difference between a child's attainment level when working alone versus working with an older, more experienced partner such as an adult

6.4 What is adolescence, and what distinguishes it as a unique stage of development?

Adolescence	- A period of development that lasts from puberty and ends with physiological maturity. - Approximately ages 9-25, later start for males - Different for each individual - Changes in sex characteristics affect body image, self-concept, and self-esteem - Cognitive abilities advance- see Piaget - Greater emphasis on social acceptance - G Stanley Hall described it as a period of "storm and stress."
Puberty	- The stage of development occurs when genital organs fully mature and secondary sex characteristics appear. - Ejaculation of sperm in males - Menarche in females - Growth of pubic hair
Menarche	The first incidence of menstruation in females marks the beginning of puberty
Primary Sex Characteristics	Testes in males and ovaries in females
Secondary Sex Characteristics	Characteristics not directly involved in reproduction, such as voice quality, facial hair, and breast size

Self-Concept	Evaluation of one's psychological self, which includes physical characteristics, skills, roles, and personal qualities
Self-Esteem	The extent that the qualities one includes in their self-concept are perceived to be positive.

6.5 What are the cognitive and physical changes of adulthood?

| Adulthood | - The period of human development when one reaches full physical, cognitive, social, and other processes fully mature and other changes associated with aging
- Sensory (vision, hearing, taste, smell) and physical attributes such as reaction time slowly worsen starting at 30 and steeply at 70. |
|---|---|
| Menopause | A biological stage of life in women when reproductive capacity decreases and stops due to changes in levels of estrogen and progesterone. Ages 45-55 |
| Alzheimer's Disease | - A neurodegenerative disease that causes dementia and other cognitive declines
- Typically occurs after the age of 70. |
| Dementia | Deterioration of memory and other cognitive functions |

Crystallized Intelligence	Knowledge of vocabulary and general information. Increases during adulthood.
Fluid Intelligence	Dealing with novel tasks. Speed decreases with aging
Social Clock	The set of norms within a culture about the ages at which life events should occur, such as school, marriage, having children and retiring.

Elisabeth Kubler-Ross's Stages of Death and Dying - moods and strategies for coping with the dying process, bereavement, and trauma. The stages do not necessarily occur in order

Denial Stage	inability to acknowledge it
Anger Stage	anger, resentment, or rage
Bargaining Stage	negotiate a deal with a God/fate
Depression Stage	sadness, regret, uncertainty
Acceptance Stage	emotional detachment, resignation to the reality of it

How do our social and psychological lives change throughout life?

Erik Erikson's Stages of Psychosocial Development

Age	Issue	Description
Infancy (birth to 1)	Trust vs. Mistrust	Needs are dependably met or not
Toddlerhood (1-2)	Autonomy vs. Shame and Doubt	Learn to do things on their own or doubt their abilities
Preschooler (3-5)	Initiative vs. Guilt	Initiate and carry out tasks independently or feel guilty about one's inability to do so
Elementary (6-puberty)	Competence vs. Inferiority	Learn the pleasure of doing tasks or feeling inferior
Adolescence (teen-20s)	Identity vs. Role Confusion	Testing roles and identities and developing a sense of self or becoming confused about who they are
Young Adulthood (20-40)	Intimacy vs. Isolation	Gain the capacity for intimate love or feel socially isolated
Middle Adulthood (40-60)	Generativity vs. Stagnation	Sense of contributions to the world or lack of purpose
Late Adulthood (60 and up)	Integrity vs. Despair	Period of reflection when one feels satisfied or a sense of failure

An important debate throughout developmental psychology is continuity versus stages. Is development a gradual and continuous process, or are there distinct stages, as many of the theorists mentioned in this unit believe?

6.6 What are the models of moral development?

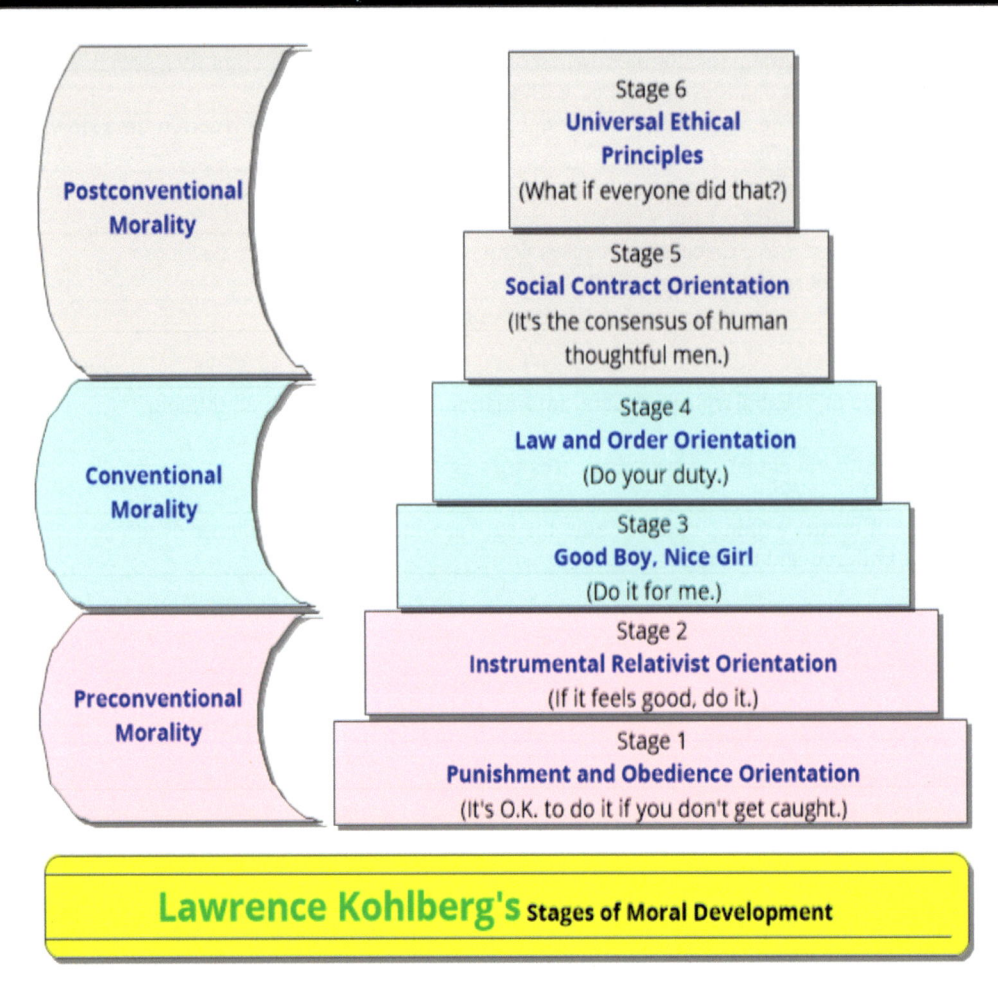

Lawrence Kohlberg's Stages of Moral Development

- **Postconventional Morality**
  - Stage 6: **Universal Ethical Principles** (What if everyone did that?)
  - Stage 5: **Social Contract Orientation** (It's the consensus of human thoughtful men.)
- **Conventional Morality**
  - Stage 4: **Law and Order Orientation** (Do your duty.)
  - Stage 3: **Good Boy, Nice Girl** (Do it for me.)
- **Preconventional Morality**
  - Stage 2: **Instrumental Relativist Orientation** (If it feels good, do it.)
  - Stage 1: **Punishment and Obedience Orientation** (It's O.K. to do it if you don't get caught.)

Carol Gilligan	<ul><li>Student of **Kohlberg**</li><li>Criticized his theory as being male-centric</li><li>Believed women reason differently by focusing more on interpersonal relationships.</li></ul>

6.7 How do gender and sex influence socialization and development?

Gender	Psychological, behavioral, social, and cultural aspects of being male or female
Sex	Physical and biological traits of males and females
Gender Identity	Self-identification as male or female
Gender Schema Theory	Beliefs and expectations about one's understanding of what it means to be male or female
Socialization	The process of acquiring social skills, beliefs, and values needed to function in a society or group.

Unit 7- Motivation, Emotion, and Personality (11-15% AP Exam Weighting)

7.1 What are the theories of motivation?

Motivation	Something that directs or energizes behavior.
Intrinsic Motivation	A desire to engage in an activity due to the pleasure in it
Extrinsic Motivation	An external incentive, reward, or punishment for engaging in a behavior
Achievement Motivation	The desire to perform well and be successful
Self-Efficacy	• An individual's perception of their ability to perform based on self-reflection and self-regulation • Albert Bandura proposed that it is a primary motivator of behavioral change.

Drive-Reduction Theory	A **physiological need** that causes a **drive** that **motivates** behavior to address the **drive state**
Need	Deprivation of something needed for survival
Drive	A state of readiness that motivates an activity
Incentives	An external stimulus that motivates behavior

Need (food, water) → **Drive** (hunger, thirst) → **Drive-Reducing Behaviors** (eating, drinking)

It is important to distinguish between a need and a drive. A need is a physiological requirement of survival, such as food, water, and air. A drive is the feeling one has when they are deprived of that need. "I feel hungry" is a drive.

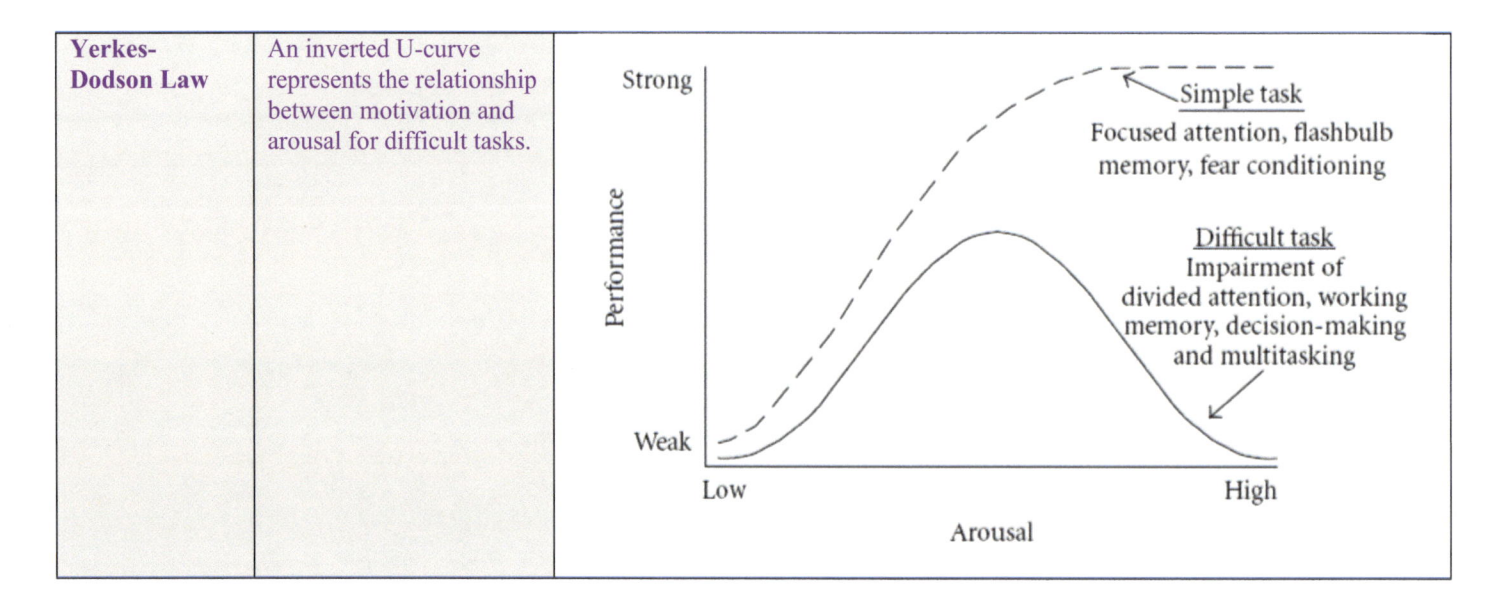

Yerkes-Dodson Law	An inverted U-curve represents the relationship between motivation and arousal for difficult tasks.	Graph: Performance (Weak to Strong) vs Arousal (Low to High). Simple task (dashed curve): Focused attention, flashbulb memory, fear conditioning. Difficult task (solid curve): Impairment of divided attention, working memory, decision-making and multitasking

Instinct	An inborn, species-specific, biological force that directs the behavior of an organism.
Evolutionary Theory of Motivation	Organisms are motivated to engage in behavior that ensures their species' survival
Arousal Theory	The physical environment can stimulate or stress to motivate behavior. Seek out things that alleviate boredom. It can be cognitive, emotional, social, psychological, or physiological.
Maslow's Hierarchy of Needs	Progression through the pyramid below motivates behavior

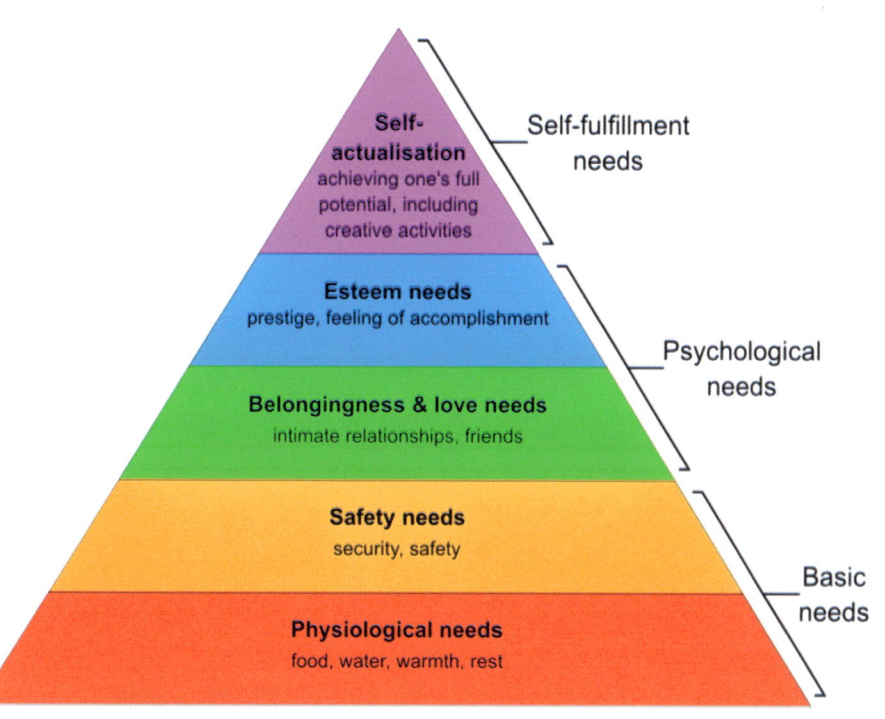

Androidmarsexpress, Maslow's Hierarchy of Needs2, CC BY-SA 4.0

| Maslow's Hierarchy of Needs | Progression through the pyramid below motivates behavior |

7.2 What are the biological motivators to eat?

Hunger	The sensation caused by the need for food
Homeostasis	The regulation of body chemistry to maintain a balanced internal state
Set Point	<ul><li>A preferred level of functioning.</li><li>Ex. Body weight has a set point.</li><li>When the body weight falls below it, there is increased hunger and a lower basal metabolic rate.</li></ul>
Settling Point	Body weight does not have a specific set point; instead, it drifts based on factors such as food consumption, energy expenditure, and genetic factors.
Basal Metabolic Rate or Metabolism	The minimum energy expenditure that is required to maintain bodily functions.
Obesity	<ul><li>The condition of having excess body fat beyond the normal BMI</li><li>Linked with poor health outcomes such as heart disease and diabetes</li></ul>
Body Mass Index (BMI)	BMI = Weight/Height squared

Hypothalamus	Part of the brain that regulates hormones related to thirst and hunger. 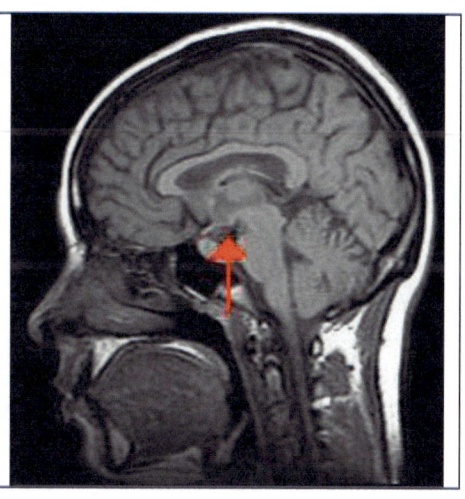
Lateral	Lesions resulted in fasting and weight loss. Stimulation of it increased food intake.
Ventromedial	Lesions resulting in overeating to obesity. Stimulation resulted in fasting

Hunger Hormones	
Ghrelin	Secreted in the stomach and stimulates appetite and the growth hormone.
Insulin	Secreted in the pancreas and it helps with the transfer of glucose through cell membranes. The absence of enough makes glucose accumulate in the blood.
Leptin	Found in the brain's hypothalamus and communicates the amount of body fat stored. It helps regulate food intake.
Orexin	Found in the hypothalamus and triggers feeding.
PYY	It is in the digestive tract and signals to the brain that one is not hungry.

Washburn Study	• Swallowed a balloon that measured stomach contractions. • Found that hunger pangs in the stomach corresponded with stomach contractions.

What are the psychological motivators to eat?

Minnesota Starvation Experiment	• **Ancel Keys** • Cut participants' caloric intake in half. • They became obsessed with food • Conversations centered around it • Read cookbooks • Lost interest in other activities

Neophobia	Fear of anything new

What are the biological, cognitive, societal, and psychological motivators of sex?

Sex Drive	An arousal state that creates a desire for sexual gratification and reproduction
Testosterone	• A male sex hormone that stimulates the male reproductive organs • Women secrete small amounts of it.
Estrogen	A female sex hormone produced by the ovaries

Sexual Response Cycle	• **Masters and Johnson Study**
	 • Four phases:
	   ○ Excitement- genitals engorge, vagina lubricates
	   ○ Plateau- excitement peaks with rising blood pressure, pulse, and breathing
	   ○ Orgasm- pleasure feeling, muscle contractions, women's helps facilitate conception.
	   ○ Resolution- The body returns to the unaroused state.
	   ○ Men enter a refractory period where they are unable to have another orgasm.

Erotic Plasticity	The degree to which situational factors shape sexual desire and behavior.
Pornography	Writings, images, or film with sexual content designed to arouse sexual response

Sexual Dysfunctions- problems in one or more phases of the **sexual response cycle**	
Erectile Dysfunction (ED)	The loss of ability to achieve an erection.
Premature Ejaculation	Ejaculation occurs with minimal sexual stimulation or earlier than desired.
Female Orgasmic Disorder	A woman has difficulty obtaining an orgasm.
Paraphilias	• Any disorder that contains unusual fantasies for sexual excitement • Ex. Pedophilia, exhibitionism, necrophilia

Sexually Transmitted	• An infection from sexual activity. • More than 20 known STDs exist • Also known as venereal diseases

Diseases (STD)	
Sexual Orientation	One's attraction to male partners, female partners, or both
Kinsey Scale	**Alfred Kinsey** created a scale to categorize an individual's sexual orientation ranging from 0 (exclusively heterosexual) to 6 (exclusively homosexual)

What social factors motivate behavior?

The Need to Belong	The desire to be part of groups, be in relationships, and be accepted by others has biological causes and follows **social norms.**
Ostracism	- A rejection or exclusion from others - It often has powerful negative consequences on psychological well-being - Research demonstrates activation of the **anterior cingulate cortex,** which is also involved in physical pain.
Social Isolation	- Voluntary or involuntary absence of contact with others - It often produces abnormal physiological and behavioral changes.

7.3 What are the theories of emotions?

Emotion	An attempt to deal with a personally significant matter through physiological responses, experience, and expressed behaviors

James-Lange Theory of Emotion	Physiological responses precede emotions.	Person sees a spider → Heart rate goes up → Interprets bodily feeling as fear

Cannon-Bard Theory of Emotion	Emotional states result from the simultaneous brain responses from brain regions that control experiencing and expressing emotions.	Person sees a spider → **Thalamus** experiences the emotion / **Hypothalamus** alerts the body → Experiences Fear

| Schacter-Singer/Two-Factor Theory of Emotion | Emotions result from a physiological response and a cognitive appraisal of that response. | Person sees a spider → Heart rate goes up → Decide situation is dangers → Experiences Fear |

| Appraisal Theory | • **Richard Lazarus**
• Cognitive appraisals precede emotional responses. | Person sees a spider → Spiders are dangerous → Heart rate goes up → Experiences Fear |

| Robert Zajonc | Some emotions happen without a cognitive appraisal. Ex. Gut feeling |
| Joseph LeDoux | • Low road v. high road
• Low road- fear stimulus proceeds from the **thalamus** to the **amygdala**. Fight or flight takes over without input from higher cognitive brain processes.
• High road- **thalamus** to the **cortex** and then to the **amygdala** |

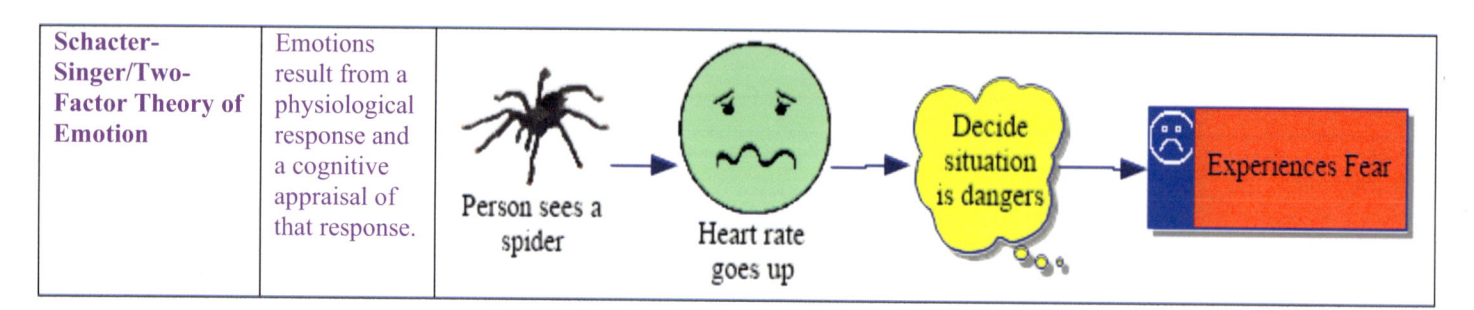

How are emotions experienced and expressed?

Polygraphs	• A device that measures physiological responses such as heart rate, blood pressure, and galvanic skin response • Lie detector- no studies indicate that it accurately detects lies from physiological responses.
Facial Feedback Effect	Facial muscle movements trigger the inner emotional states.
Body Language	Expressing emotions through posture, gestures, or movement
Display Rules	A socially learned rule that regulates how one expresses emotions.

| Feel-Good, Do-Good phenomenon | People tend to be more helpful when they are in a good mood. |

Subjective Well-Being	An appraisal of one's level of happiness and well-being based on feelings and thoughts about life
Adaptation Level Phenomenon	• A base point at which people evaluate new stimuli • The base point changes. • Ex. Someone's base level of $50,000 a year income is happy with a raise of $5,000. Eventually, $55,000 becomes the new base point.
Relative Deprivation Principle	The perception that the amount of resources (money, social status, material items) someone has is less than some other comparison.
Catharsis	The strong release of pent-up emotions

Facial Expressions	• A nonverbal signal using the facial muscles • Paul Ekman- cross-cultural research shows that some facial expressions are spontaneous and exist worldwide. • surprise, fear, anger, sadness, and happiness

7.4 What is stress, and how does it manifest?

Stress	• The physiological and psychological response to internal or external stressors • It can cause many illnesses such as anxiety disorders, heart disease, headaches, and viral infections. • Fight or flight response with release of epinephrine (adrenaline).
Cortisol	Stress hormone. Sustained levels weaken the immune system.
Stressor	Anything that results in stress
Coping Strategies	Cognitive and behavioral strategies to manage situations that exceed resources and negative emotions caused by stress

Motivational Conflicts Theory	• Kurt Lewin • A conflict or stressor with two or more goals with incompatible alternatives that exist simultaneously	• Three approaches	
		Approach-Approach- choosing between two desirable goals or motives.	
		Avoidance-Avoidance- choosing between two undesirable goals or motives.	
		Approach-Avoidance- choosing between a goal or motive with desirable and undesirable consequences.	
General Adaptation Syndrome	• The physiological stress response. • Hans Selye 1. Alarm- increase in sympathetic nervous system arousal. 2. Resistance- stabilization of increased sympathetic nervous system arousal 3. Exhaustion- breakdown with symptoms such as sleep loss, irritability, and fatigue.	David G. Myers, General Adaptation Syndrome, CC BY 3.0	

7.5 What is personality?

Personality	• A complex dynamic of individual characteristics, traits, drives, self-concept, abilities, and emotions that help determine behavior. • Competing theories about what it is and how to study it

How do researchers study personality?

```
                    Study of
                   Personality
              ↙        ↓        ↘
      Case Study   Surveys   Personality
                             Inventories
           ↓          ↓           ↓
      Observe,    Large and   Self reported
      interview   random      traits and
      and         sample      behaviors. Can
      describe    can be      use to find
      individuals more        correlations
      or small    representa- to other items.
      groups      tive of a
                  population
```

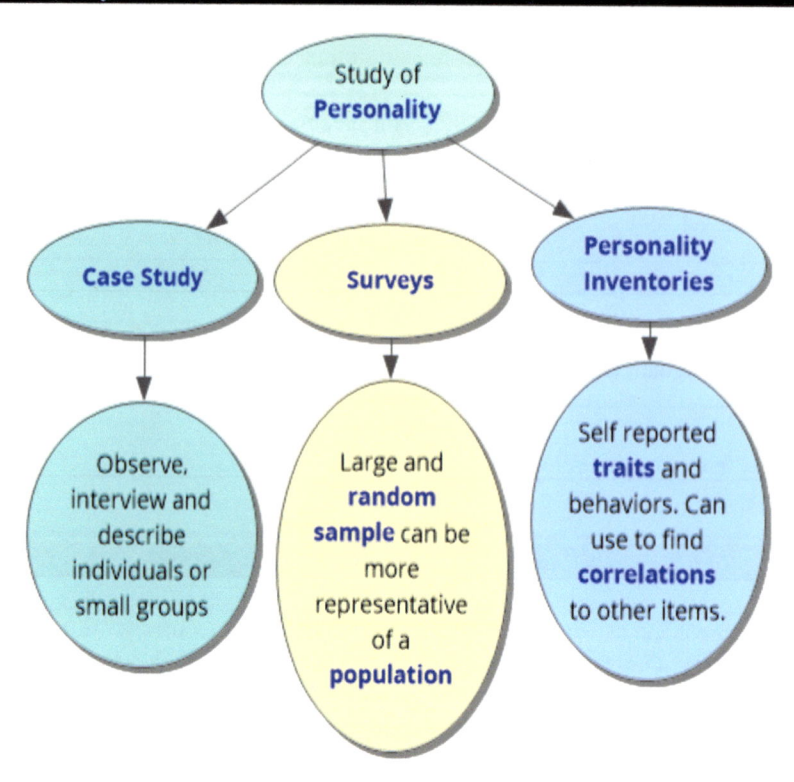

7.6 What is Sigmund Freud's psychoanalytic theory, and how does it differ from other theories?

Psychoanalytic Perspective	• **Sigmund Freud-** Physician who did **case studies** • The primary assumption is that much of mental activity is **unconscious,** and to understand people, one needs to determine the meaning of it.
Unconscious	The memories, emotional conflicts, and internal struggles that are not accessible to awareness still affect thoughts and behavior.
Preconscious	The mental states that our outside awareness can be accessed and brought to awareness upon command.
Conscious	The memories, thoughts, feelings, and other aspects of mental life in awareness

(Iceberg diagram: Conscious above water; Preconscious, Ego, Superego, Id, Unconscious below)

Personality Structure	• The primary traits and components of personality • In **Freud**'s theory, it consists of the **id, ego,** and **superego**

Id	• The aspect of **personality** that contains instinctual, biological **drives**
	• Has the **libido** and operates by the **pleasure principle**.
	Libido- sexual instinct, pleasure, and expressions of love.
	Pleasure Principle-
	  • The desire for gratification or pleasure
	  • Tension builds when gratification is lacking.

Ego	• The aspect of **personality** that deals with the external world and its practical demands • It is the mediator between the **id** and **superego**.
Superego	The aspect of **personality** that regulates right and wrong based on parental and societal standards.

Psychoanalysis	• An approach to the mind and **psychological disorders** • Attempts to understand and interpret **unconscious** mental activity
Free Association	• When a patient verbalizes, without a filter, whatever thoughts come to mind, even if they are embarrassing or illogical • Allows the **unconscious** to slip to the surface.
Dream Analysis	Analyzing the content of dreams (**manifest content**) for underlying motivations and symbolic meanings (**latent content**)
Manifest Content	The recalled images and events of a dream
Latent Content	The hidden and disguised meanings, desires, and conflicts that the dreamers' mind represents as images and events in dreams

Freud's Psychosexual Stages- the sexual development of an individual that affects personality. The **libido** focuses on different organs.

Stage	Focus	Results
Oral (0-18 months)	The mouth is the erotic zone, and one receives gratification from sucking during feeding.	**Oral Personality**- Satisfied = friendly and optimistic. Unsatisfied = hostile and critical. **Oral Fixation/Oral Eroticism**- pleasure derived from oral activities such as smoking, biting, kissing, etc.
Anal (18-36 months)	The expulsion of feces is the focus of gratification.	**Anal Personality**- Satisfied = frugality and order. Unsatisfied = aggressive and defiance
Phallic (3-6 years)	The genital area is the focus of gratification.	Boys have **castration anxiety**. Experience the **Oedipus Complex**. Girls have **penis envy**.
Latency (6-puberty)	Sexual interest wanes in favor of peer activities.	Transitional stage
Genital (puberty on)	**Oedipus complex** resolves, and the focus is on intercourse.	Satisfaction = true intimacy and concern for partner's satisfaction.

Oedipus Complex	• Erotic feelings of a son towards his mother • Hostility towards father and fear of castration • Gradual **identification** with father
Identification	Associating the self with others
Fixation	Stuck in an early stage of **psychosexual development**

Defense Mechanisms- unconscious reaction by the ego to protect from anxiety	
Repression	Pushing painful experiences out of **consciousness**
Regression	Return to an earlier stage of development
Reaction Formation	Replacing **Unconscious** impulses with the **conscious** opposite
Projection	Attributing one's characteristics and impulses to another person or group
Rationalization	Giving logical reasons to justify unacceptable behavior, thoughts, and **unconscious** impulses
Displacement	Transferring feelings from the original object or person to some other thing or person
Sublimation	**Unconsciously** channeling unacceptable drives and impulses into socially acceptable behaviors

Study Tip- Elaboration/Deep Processing/Semantic Encoding: As you go through your day, identify times that you or others used each of the defense mechanisms above. Ex. You recognize that you are rationalizing when thinking it would be okay to cheat on a test because everyone is doing it.

Terror-Management Theory	Using **defense mechanisms** to relieve death anxiety
Collective Unconscious	• **Carl Jung** • Common to all humans is a collection of inherited ideas and images called **archetypes**. • The deepest part of the **unconscious**
Inferiority Complex	• **Alfred Adler** • A feeling of inadequacy and insecurity • He believed this was the most significant source of inner conflict during childhood

Projective Tests	An assessment with unambiguous stimuli to determine unconscious thoughts, personality traits, and thought processes	
Rorschach Inkblot Test	• **Hermann Rorschach** • A **projective test** that utilizes ten inkblots of random design	
Thematic Apperception Test	A **projective test** that asks participants to create a written story about black-and-white pictures	

7.7 What are the social-cognitive theories of personality?

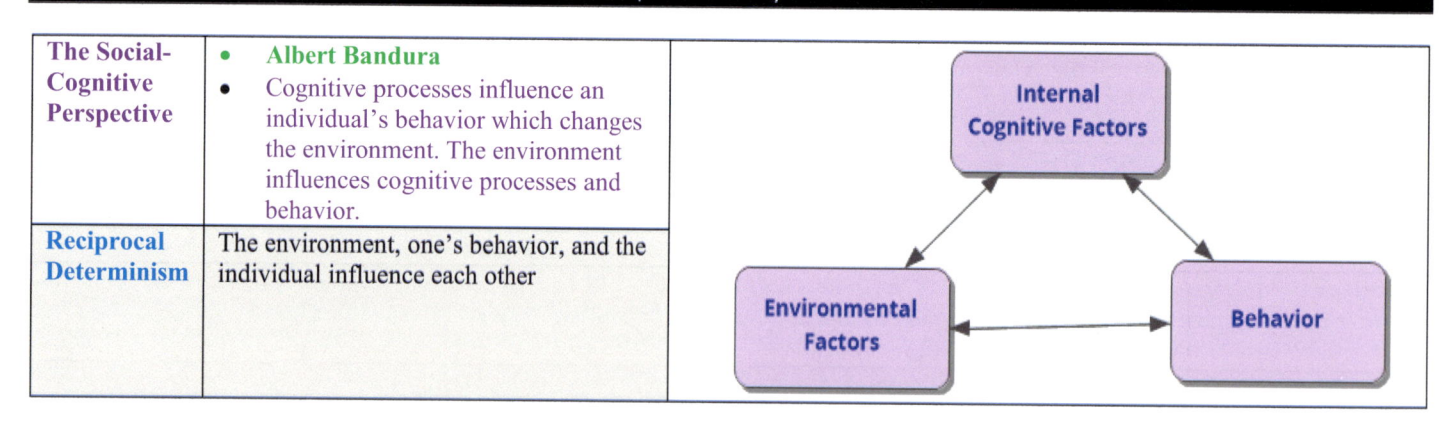

The Social-Cognitive Perspective	• **Albert Bandura** • Cognitive processes influence an individual's behavior which changes the environment. The environment influences cognitive processes and behavior.
Reciprocal Determinism	The environment, one's behavior, and the individual influence each other

(Diagram: Internal Cognitive Factors ↔ Environmental Factors ↔ Behavior)

Personal Control	The feeling of power and influence over events, behaviors, and people
Internal Locus of Control	Behavior and corresponding belief that life outcomes result from one's abilities.
External Locus of Control	Behavior and the corresponding belief that life outcomes result from factors outside one's control.

Learned Helplessness	Repeated exposure to uncontrollable **stressors** causes individuals not to attempt control even when options become available. -**Overmier and Seligman** administered electric shocks to a harnessed dog and found that the dog later did not attempt to escape the shocks after they removed the harness.

Rose M. Spielman, Ph.D., Shuttle Box Dog Orange, CC BY 4.0

Spotlight Effect	The overestimation is that others notice and evaluate one's appearance, performance, and foibles more than they actually pay attention.
Optimists	People who anticipate positive outcomes.
Pessimists	People who expect bad things to happen to them or others.

7.8 What is the humanistic perspective of personality?

Humanistic Perspective	• **Abraham Maslow** and **Carl Rogers** • The belief is that people are good and want to reach their full potential (self-actualization).

Self-Actualization	• **Abraham Maslow** • People can reach their full potential, maximum abilities, and appreciation for life once the needs of survival, safety, love, belongingness, and esteem are fulfilled.

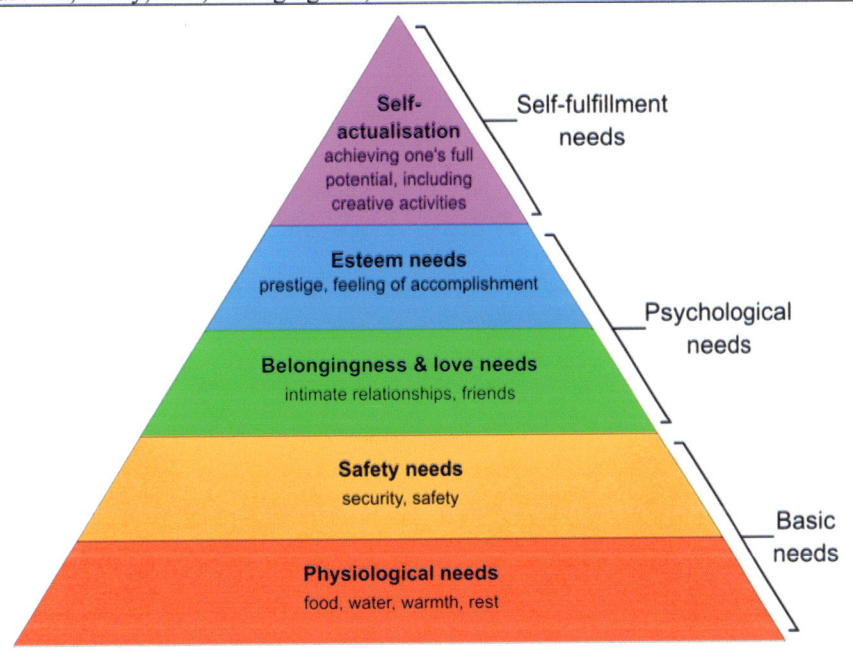

Maslow's Hierarchy of Needs pyramid:
- Self-actualisation: achieving one's full potential, including creative activities (Self-fulfillment needs)
- Esteem needs: prestige, feeling of accomplishment (Psychological needs)
- Belongingness & love needs: intimate relationships, friends (Psychological needs)
- Safety needs: security, safety (Basic needs)
- Physiological needs: food, water, warmth, rest (Basic needs)

Androidmarsexpress, Maslow's Hierarchy of Needs2, CC BY-SA 4.0

Unconditional Positive Regard	• **Carl Rogers** • An attitude of (1) acceptance, (2) empathy, and (3) genuineness toward others regardless of their behavior • He believed it was essential for healthy development.

Positive Psychology	• **Martin E.P. Seligman** • How to live a worthwhile life • Focuses on what is good and how reach it instead of negatives. • Examines how psychological states such happiness combined with personality traits and societal forces can interact to increase one's overall subjective well-being.

What are the differences between individualistic and collectivist cultures?

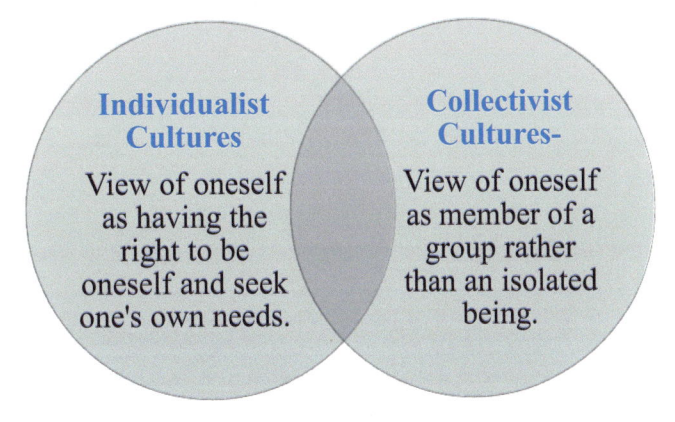

Individualist Cultures: View of oneself as having the right to be oneself and seek one's own needs.

Collectivist Cultures: View of oneself as member of a group rather than an isolated being.

7.9 What are the similarities and differences of the trait theories?

Traits	Characteristics of personality that determine an individual's behavior
Allport's Personality Trait Theory	• Gordon Allport • An individual's personality traits are crucial to understanding behavior.
Personality Inventory	An objectively scored assessment in which individuals respond to statements or questions about themselves.

The Myers-Briggs Type Indicator (MBTI)	• A personality inventory based on Jungian typology (Carl Jung) of extraversion vs. introversion, sensing vs. intuition, thinking vs. feeling, and judging vs. perceiving • The test assigns participants four letters (ex. ESTJ) and a description of their personality type. • Not used or considered valid by research psychologists. • Many organizations and counseling services use them.
Sixteen Personality Factor Inventory (16PF)	• Raymond Cattell • A personality inventory that assesses 16 key scales • Warmth, vigilance, reasoning, abstractness, emotional stability, privateness, dominance, apprehension, liveliness, openness, rule-consciousness, self-reliance, social boldness, perfectionism, sensitivity, and tension.
Eysenck Personality Inventory Or Questionnaire (EPI or EPQ)	• Hans and Sybil Eysenck • A self-report personality inventory that measures on two dimensions and a lie scale • Extraversion versus Introversions • Stable versus Unstable
The Minnesota Multiphasic Personality Inventory (MMPI)	• A self-report personality inventory that is by mental health and forensics experts • Empirically derived

The Big Five Personality Inventory	• Paul Costa and Robert McCrae
	• A personality inventory that measures five dimensions
	    O – Openness
	    C – Conscientiousness
	    E – Extraversion
	    A – Agreeableness
	    N – Neuroticism
	• Widely used by research psychologists.

The Person-Situation Controversy	• The debate about the persistency of traits across different situations • Trait theorists argue it is the average behavior.

7.10 How are traits measured?

Factor Analysis	A mathematical procedure for reducing the number of variables by determining correlations
Empirically Derived	A mathematical procedure is used in assessments in which answers are scored to determine difference in responses among groups known to differ.

Unit 8- Clinical Psychology (12-16% AP Exam Weighting)

8.1 How do psychologists and psychiatrists diagnose mental illnesses?

Abnormal Behavior	<ul><li>Behavior that is atypical within a culture, maladaptive, or determinantal to an individual.</li><li>Deviant, distressful, and dysfunctional</li><li>Evidence of a mental illness</li></ul>
Deviant	Breaking the social norms established for a group
Distressful	A negative emotional state that causes changes in physiological activity
Dysfunctional	An impairment or disturbance of behavior

Medical Model	<ul><li>First advocated by Philippe Pinel and then later by Dorthea Dix</li><li>Equating mental or emotional problems to biological problems with specific causes, diagnosis, doctors, hospitals, and prescribed treatments.</li></ul>
Mental Illness or Mental Disorder	Cognitive or emotional disturbances, abnormal behaviors, impaired functioning, or any combination
Comorbidity	The presence of more than one illness, disease, or disorder simultaneously
Diagnostic and Statistical Manual of Mental Disorders, Fifth Edition, Text Revision (DSM-5-TR)	<ul><li>Published by the American Psychiatric Association as the means of diagnosing disorders</li><li>Descriptions of diagnostic categories</li><li>Hundreds of disorders</li><li>The text revision added a new disorder called prolonged grief disorder and codes for suicidal behavior and nonsuicidal injury</li></ul>

*** Before the medical model, people with abnormal behavior were often labeled as "crazy" or "insane" and placed in asylums, which often involved inhumane treatment.***

How does mental illness impact the legal system?

Confidentiality	A principle of mental health care providers or medical care that limits the disclosure of personal information shared by the patient, such as their identity, condition, diagnosis, and treatment
Insanity Defense	A plea in a criminal case that the individual lacks responsibility because of the condition of their mind at the time of the crime.

8.2 What are the strengths and limitations of explaining psychological disorders?

Etiology	The systematic scientific study of the causes of illnesses and disorders		
Approach to Etiology	**Strength**		**Limitations**
Biological- a physical, chemical, genetic, or neurological cause of disturbances	<ul><li>Some disorders show a genetic trace</li><li>Brain studies show differences in structure and functioning</li><li>Medicine is a treatment option</li></ul>		<ul><li>It does not include stressors, cognitive factors, learning, and environmental influences</li></ul>
The Diathesis Stress Model- mental disorders develop from genetics, biology (diathesis) in combination with stressful conditions.	<ul><li>It incorporates both nature and nurture</li><li>Multiple causes</li></ul>		<ul><li>Some disorders develop in individuals without the environmental factors</li></ul>
Epigenetics- Examines how genes turn on or off from environmental conditions.	<ul><li>Identical twin studies show that sometimes only one of the twins gets a disease.</li></ul>		<ul><li>It discounts the cognitive factors of illness</li></ul>

What are the benefits and drawbacks of diagnostic labels?

Benefits	Drawbacks
Reliability of diagnosis by different professionals	**Rosenhan Study-** <ul><li>He and seven other participants presented themselves to mental hospitals and said they heard voices which was a lie.</li><li>The institution admitted all the participants and prescribed them medication</li><li>Staff interpreted normal behavior as part of their illness</li></ul>
Helpful for communication among health care providers	May stigmatize
Allows for the suggestion of treatment	Can be subjective
A common language for researchers	Confirmation bias
Can study for causes	No total agreement

8.3 What are the major neurodevelopmental and schizophrenic spectrum disorders? What are their symptoms?

Neurodevelopmental Disorders- First diagnosed in childhood and includes developmental problems in academics, intellectual, and social functioning.

Types and Description	Symptoms
Attention-Deficit/Hyperactivity Disorder (ADHD) is a combination of problems such as difficulty sustaining attention, hyperactivity, and impulsive behavior.	**Inattention-** ignores details, makes careless mistakes in schoolwork, appears not to listen, has difficulty organizing tasks, and is easily distracted. **Hyperactivity-** fidgets, squirms, taps feet, on the go, talks too much, difficulty waiting for their turn, interrupts others
Autism Spectrum Disorder (ASD) is related to brain development and impacts how the person socializes, repetitive behaviors with a wide range of severity.	Poor eye contact, resists cuddling and holding, delayed speech, speaks in abnormal tone or rhythm, repeats things, doesn't express emotions, unaware of others' feelings, difficulty recognizing nonverbal cues
Learning Disability Information processing problems in people with average to above average intelligence	Difficulty reading, writing, doing simple math, problems with memory, and visual-spatial skills
Intellectual Disability Limitations in cognitive function typical for one's age group	Difficulty learning, problem-solving, reasoning, planning, and adaptive behavior.

Neurocognitive Disorders- decreased mental functioning due to a medical disease.

Type and Description	Symptoms
Dementia Deterioration of memory and a minimum of one other cognitive functions	Memory loss, difficulty finding words, trouble with visual and spatial abilities, difficulty planning, confusion, disorientation

Psychotic Disorders- Severe mental disorders that manifest as impairment in reality

Type and Description	Symptoms
Schizophrenic Spectrum or Schizophrenia Disturbances in thinking, emotional response, and behavior	**Delusions-** a personal belief, conviction, or idea that one's culture rejects **Hallucinations-** A false perception without an external stimulus. Auditory and visual are the most common. **Disorganized Speech-** incoherent speech, ideas shift, illogical, made-up words. **Catatonic Behavior-** muscular rigidity, bizarre postures- it is a **negative symptom** because behavior is subtracted.

8.4 What are the major anxiety and depressive disorders? What are their symptoms?

Anxiety Disorder- Group of disorders characterized by fear and worry	
Types and Description	**Symptoms**
Phobia Persistent fear of a specific activity, object, or situation	Intense fear is out of proportion to actual risk, avoidance, and physical reactions such as sweating, chest tightness, and difficulty breathing.
Panic Disorder Characterized by panic attacks	**Panic attack-** intense fear with heart palpitations, difficulty breathing, chest pain, smothering sensations, sweating, and dizziness. Concern with having another panic attack and worrying about the consequences of them.
Generalized Anxiety Disorder (GAD) Excessive worry	Occurs "more days than not" for six months or more. Restlessness, fatigue, impaired concentration, and disturbed sleep. Difficult to control
Obsessive-Compulsive Disorder (OCD) Recurrent intrusive thoughts that prompt performance rituals to alleviate them.	**Obsessions-** a persistent and often intrusive thought that causes anxiety and distress **Compulsions-** a type of behavior or mental act to reduce anxiety and stress
Posttraumatic Stress Disorder (PTSD) May result when an individual experiences or witnesses an event that is a threat to life and safety	Reexperiencing the trauma, flashbacks, recurring nightmares, avoidance of activities associated with the event, startle responses, disturbed sleep, difficulty concentrating, survivor guilt

Mood Disorders- prolonged and pervasive emotional disturbances	
Types and Description	**Symptoms**
Major Depressive Disorder Persistent sadness	Sadness, angry outbursts, loss of interest in usual activities, sleep disturbances, lack of energy, reduced appetite, anxiety, feelings of worthlessness, unexplained physical problems
Dysthymic Disorder Sadness that is less severe but more enduring	Loss of interest in everyday activities, sadness, hopelessness, sleep problems, low self-esteem, and trouble concentrating.
Seasonal Affective Disorder (SAD) Depressive episodes occur at certain times of the year-usually the fall or winter	Sadness most of the day, loss of interest in usual activities, feeling sluggish, sleeping too much, carbohydrate cravings, feeling hopeless, weight gain
Bipolar Disorder I and II Depression alternates with mania (I) or hypomania (II).	**Depression** symptoms are the same as those listed above. **Mania-** abnormally upbeat, jumpy, agitated, easily exaggerated sense of well-being and self-confidence, decreased need for sleep, talkative, racing thoughts, poor decision-making.

8.5 What are the major somatic and dissociative disorders? What are their symptoms?

Somatoform Disorder- symptoms in the body despite no evidence of biological problems.	
Types and Description	**Symptoms**
Illness Anxiety Disorder, formerly called **Hypochondriasis** Preoccupation with the fear or belief that one has a severe physical disease.	Preoccupation with getting a severe disease, worrying that minor symptoms are something more serious, doctors' visits does not reduce feelings, hard to function due to distress about illness, frequent medical appointments, frequently searching the internet
Somatic Disorder Bodily symptoms that cause distress without the presence of a medical condition	It includes specific sensations such as pain without the presence of a medical condition. Thoughts about the illness make it difficult to function (same as above).
Body Dysmorphic Disorder (BDD) Preoccupation with an imagined body defect or slight body anomaly	Attempts to hide or fix the perceived bodily flaw, constantly comparing appearance to others, perfectionist tendencies, avoiding social situations.

Dissociative Disorders- disruption in the integration of consciousness, memory, and perception of the environment	
Types and Description	Symptoms
Dissociative Identity Disorder (DID) It includes the presence of two or more identities in one individual. It is associated with physical or sexual abuse typically during childhood.	There are two or more identities, each with their perception of themselves and the world and gaps in memory. Symptoms are not related to drugs or other medical conditions.
Dissociative Amnesia Failure to recall important information from personal experiences	One or more episodes of an inability to recall important personal information, identity, or life history. Fugue- travel or confused wandering with amnesia.
Depersonalization Disorder One or more episodes of detachment from self that impairs social functioning	Feelings of being detached from oneself, an outside observer of self, aware that the experience is not reality, feelings of a dream world

8.6 What are the major eating, substance, addictive, and personality disorders? What are their symptoms?

Eating Disorder- disturbance in attitudes and behaviors related to food.	
Types and Description	Symptoms
Anorexia Nervosa The persistent refusal of food, excessive fear of weight gain, and disturbed body image	Extreme weight loss, thin appearance, fatigue, insomnia, dizziness and fainting, hair thins and falls out, absence of menstruation, abdominal pain, dry or yellowish skin, intolerance to cold, low blood pressure, dehydration, swelling of arms and legs,
Bulimia Nervosa Episodes of binge eating followed by behaviors to rid the food	Preoccupation with body shape and weight, binge eating, forcing vomit, exercising too much, using laxatives, diuretics, or enemas after food, fasting, and dietary supplements.
Binge-Eating Disorder Uncontrolled consumption of large quantities of food and accompanying distress of it	An excessive amount of food at one time, eating behavior is out of control, eating when not hungry, eating alone or in secret, depression, disgust or shame, and frequent dieting.

Personality Disorder- Pervasive thinking related to self and environment that interferes with functioning	
Types and Description	Symptoms
Schizoid Personality Disorder Emotional coldness and lack of feelings for others and relationships	Wanting to be alone, not enjoying or wanting close relationships, feeling like one can't experience pleasure, difficulty expressing emotions seems humorless, emotionally cold, and don't react to praise or criticism.
Borderline Personality Disorder Instability of mood, interpersonal relations, and self-image	Intense fear of abandonment, unstable relationships, idealizing people and then suddenly thinking they are cruel, rapid changes to identity, impulsive, risky behavior, suicidal threats or self-injury, mood swings, intense anger, and physical fights.
Narcissistic Personality Disorder Grandiose self-importance	An exaggerated sense of self-importance requires constant and excessive admiration, expects to be recognized as superior, exaggerates achievements and talents, fantasies of success/power/brilliance/beauty, only associates with others who are superior, monopolizes conversations, expect special favors, takes advantage of others, arrogant, boastful.
Antisocial Personality Disorder Demonstrate little regard for right and wrong and the feelings of others. Sometimes called sociopathy or psychopathy.	Breaking the law, manipulating others, deceitfulness, impulsivity, lack of guilt, remorse, and empathy. Superficial charm, aggresiveness

Substance Use Disorder Substance use with social, legal, occupational, or interpersonal consequences: alcohol, amphetamines, cannabis, cocaine, hallucinogens, opioids, nicotine, and other drugs.	Feeling that one has to use the drug regularly, having intense urges, needing more of it, maintaining a supply, spending money on it that one can't afford, not meeting obligations, continued use even with the problems it causes, driving while impaired, failing in attempts to stop using, experiencing withdrawal when one stops taking it.

8.7 What are the major treatment orientations for mental illness, and who is responsible for their development?

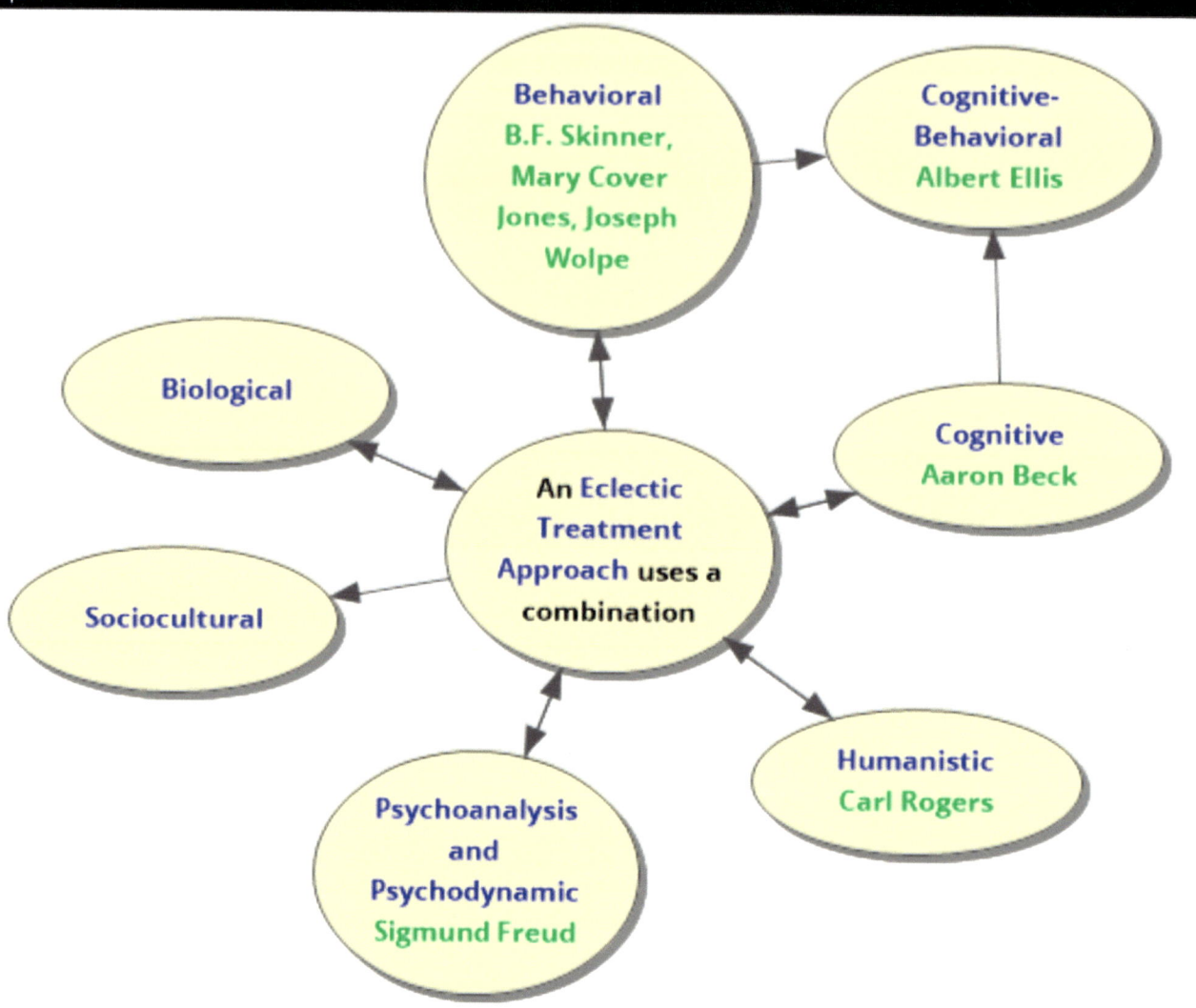

- **Behavioral** — B.F. Skinner, Mary Cover Jones, Joseph Wolpe
- **Cognitive-Behavioral** — Albert Ellis
- **Cognitive** — Aaron Beck
- **Humanistic** — Carl Rogers
- **Psychoanalysis and Psychodynamic** — Sigmund Freud
- **Sociocultural**
- **Biological**

An Eclectic Treatment Approach uses a combination

Psychotherapy	Any psychological service provided by a trained professional that uses communication to diagnose and treat mental illness or mental well-being
Psychoanalysis	• **Sigmund Freud** • Uses methods to interpret **unconscious** mental activity. • Uses **free association** • **Resistance** - blocking from consciousness any unwanted anxiety-inducing thoughts • **Dream Interpretation** • **Transference** - take emotions and place them onto the therapist. • Hard to prove or disprove scientifically • It can take a long time

Secretlondon, Freud's couch in Freud museum, CC BY-SA 4.0
Freud's Couch

***Study Tip*- Spacing Effect**: Psychoanalysis is based on the theories developed by Sigmund Freud in Unit 7: Psychoanalytic Theories of Personalities. Go back to review them because it will help you understand the therapy better.

Psychodynamic	- Similar to **psychoanalysis.** - Patients sit face-to-face. - Looks for themes in important relationships
Interpersonal Psychotherapy	- Type of psychotherapy - Time-limited - Based on the belief that relationships with others are the primary motivator of behavior.

Humanistic Therapy	- Rejects **psychoanalysis** - Foster growth and human potential in the here and now. - **Unconditional positive regard**
Client-Centered Therapy	- **Carl Rogers** - Type of **Humanistic Therapy** - Non-judgmental - Uses **Active Listening-** clarifying questions, restating patients' thoughts, and reflecting feelings

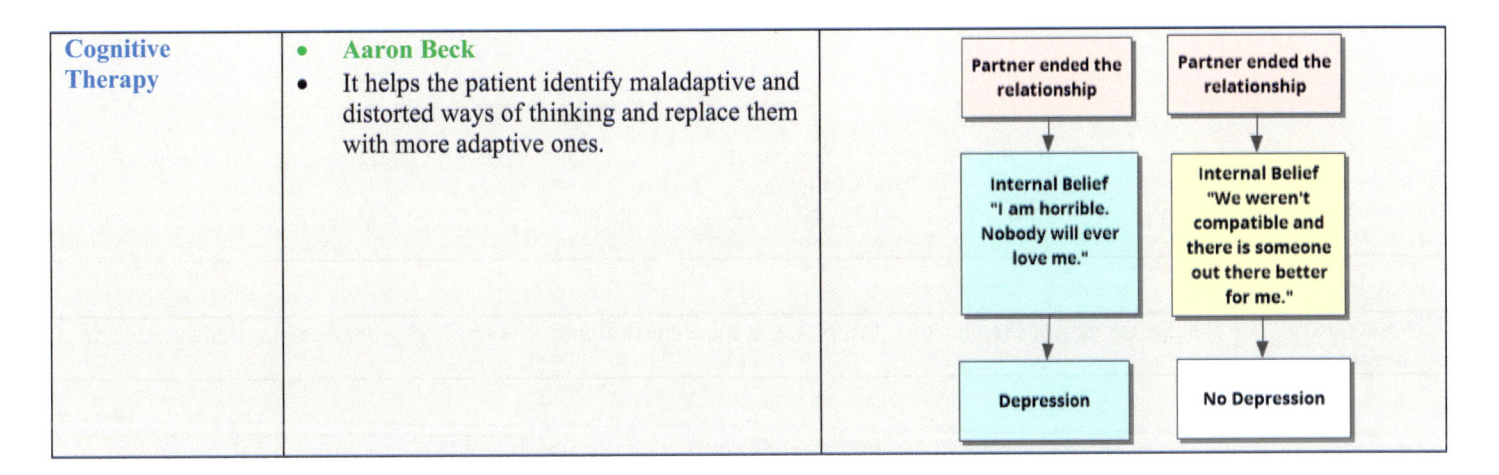

Cognitive Therapy	- **Aaron Beck** - It helps the patient identify maladaptive and distorted ways of thinking and replace them with more adaptive ones.	*Diagram: "Partner ended the relationship" leading to two paths — Internal Belief "I am horrible. Nobody will ever love me." → Depression; Internal Belief "We weren't compatible and there is someone out there better for me." → No Depression*

Behavior Therapy	- Uses **classical** and **operant conditioning** to eliminate or modify maladaptive patterns of behavior.

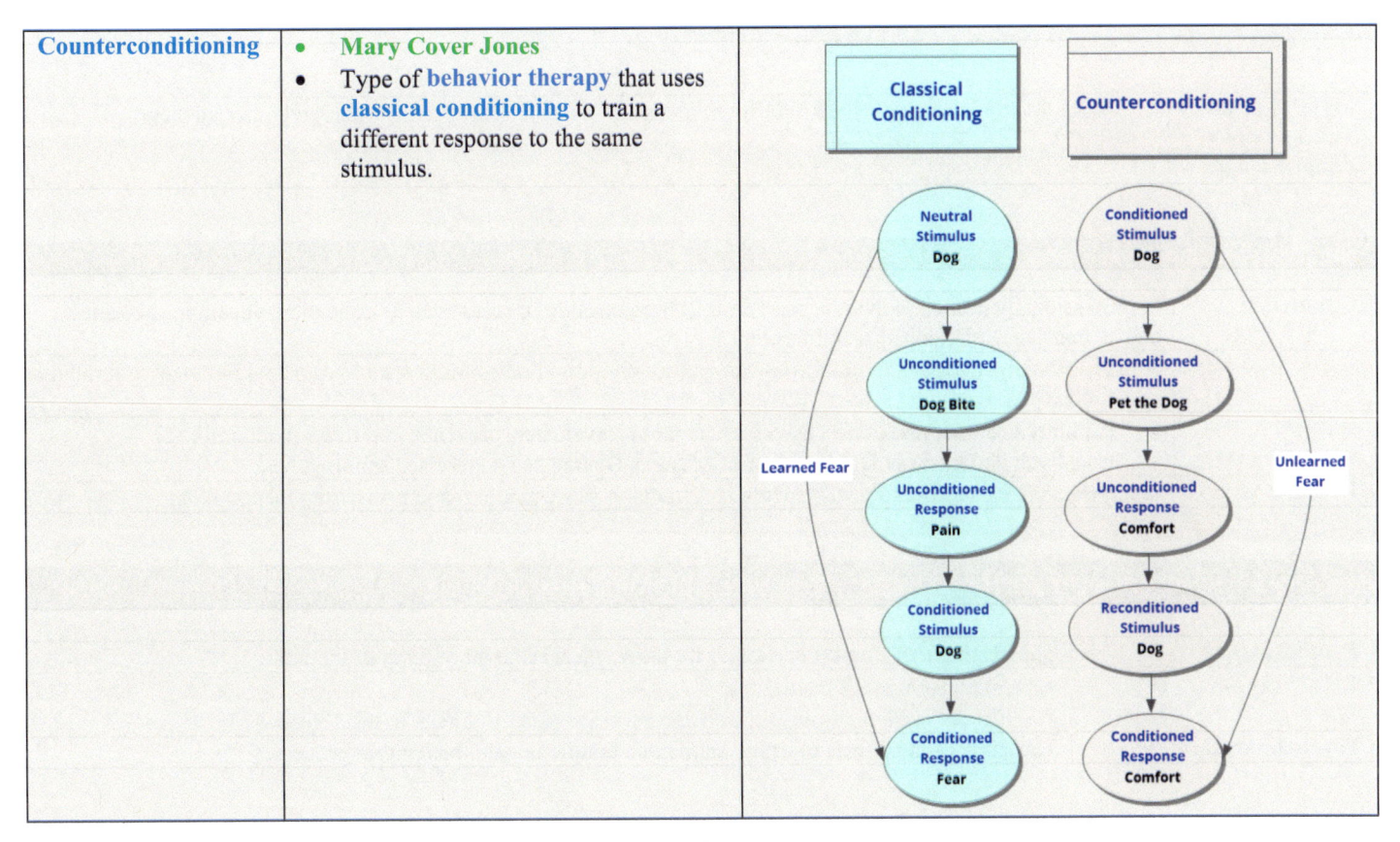

Counterconditioning	- **Mary Cover Jones** - Type of **behavior therapy** that uses **classical conditioning** to train a different response to the same stimulus.	*Diagram comparing Classical Conditioning (Neutral Stimulus: Dog → Unconditioned Stimulus: Dog Bite → Unconditioned Response: Pain → Conditioned Stimulus: Dog → Conditioned Response: Fear — Learned Fear) with Counterconditioning (Conditioned Stimulus: Dog → Unconditioned Stimulus: Pet the Dog → Unconditioned Response: Comfort → Reconditioned Stimulus: Dog → Conditioned Response: Comfort — Unlearned Fear)*

Exposure Therapy	A **behavior therapy** used for **anxiety disorders** that involve repeated confrontation with a **fear stimulus**
Systematic Desensitization	• **Joseph Wolpe** • A type of **exposure therapy** that uses counterconditioning. • Reduces **anxiety** by training the client in deep-muscle relaxation followed by gradually facing fears. • Proceed up an **anxiety hierarchy** from least to most threatening fear-inducing stimuli or situations.
Aversive or Aversion Conditioning Therapy	A type of **behavior therapy** involves an unpleasant stimulus paired with undesired behavior.

Token Economy	A **behavior therapy** that uses **operant conditioning** techniques of **reinforcing** desired behavior with tokens that participants can exchange for desirable rewards

Cognitive Behavior Therapy (CBT)	A type of **psychotherapy** that incorporates treatment techniques of **cognitive therapy** and **behavior therapy**.
Rational Emotive Behavior Therapy (REBT)	• **Albert Ellis** • A form of **CBT** that focuses on self-defeating beliefs and the negative feelings that ensue from them. • Participants integrate thinking, feeling, and acting. • The therapist helps interrupt the patient's irrational beliefs and act more self-enhancing.

Sociocultural Therapy	It helps the patient examine their symptoms in the context of their cultural background and the context of their family.

Group Therapy	A type of psychotherapy that includes two or more participants interacting in the presence of a therapist

Family Therapy	A type of psychotherapy that focuses on improving family relationships.

Light Exposure Therapy or Phototherapy	Exposure to ultraviolet or infrared light for depression, seasonal affective disorder, and other medical conditions

Who treats psychological illnesses?

Counselors	A professionally trained individual can administer counseling in areas such as education, vocation, substance abuse, marriage, relationships, and family.
Social Workers	A professionally trained individual who can work with individuals, families, and groups within their community and context
Clinical Psychologists	• An individual that researches, assesses, diagnoses, evaluates, prevents, and treats mental illness. • Usually, a Ph.D. or Psy.D. Minimum of Master's Degree and supervised training.
Psychiatrists	A physician (Medical Doctor, MD) specializes in diagnosing, treating, and preventing mental illness.

8.8 What treatment options for mental illness use a biological approach?

Psychosurgery	The treatment of **mental disorders** by the surgical removal of parts of the brain
Lobotomy	• An incision in the frontal lobes • It is not used much since the advent of **antipsychotic drugs** in the 1950s.
Psychopharmacology	The study of the effects of drugs on mental, emotional, and behavioral processes

Disorder	Treatment Type	Side Effects
Schizophrenia	- Antipsychotic Drugs- Thorazine and Chlorpromazine for positive symptoms. - Clozapine for negative symptoms. - Blocks dopamine receptors	Tardive Dyskinesia (movement disorder) twitches, tremors
Anxiety Disorders	- Antianxiety drugs- Xanax, Ativan, Marijuana - Depresses the central nervous system, - Elevates GABA	Addictive withdrawal symptoms
Mood Disorders such as Depression	- Antidepressants (SSRI)- Prozac, Zoloft, Paxil - Blocks the reuptake of serotonin and norepinephrine	Dry mouth, weight gain, hypertension, dizzy spells
Severe Depression	Electroconvulsive Therapy (ECT)	Memory Loss
Severe Depression	Repetitive Transcranial Magnetic Stimulation	Headaches
Bipolar	Lithium and Depakote	Thyroid and renal dysfunction

Unit 9- Social Psychology (8-10% AP Exam Weighting)

9.1 How do people attribute behavior, and how does it impact one's perception of the world?

Attribution Theory	• **Fritz Heider** • The process of ascribing the reason for others' behavior as either due to their disposition or the external circumstances of their situation	
Dispositional Attribution	The process of ascribing the reason for behavior to internal or psychological causes such as mood, personality, or effort	
Situational Attribution	The process of ascribing the reason for behavior to causes outside the person, such as luck, other people, or external circumstances	
Fundamental Attribution Error	The tendency of people to overestimate the degree to which **dispositional attributes** instead of **situational attributes** determine behavior.	
Actor-Observer Bias	The tendency of people to attribute their behavior to situational attributes instead of dispositional attributes, but observers do the opposite making the **fundamental attribution error**.	
Attitudes and Actions	A reciprocal relationship between a cognitive evaluation of one's surroundings and behavior	Attitudes- how one attributes ↔ Actions

Self-Serving Bias	Interpreting events that ascribe success to oneself but deny responsibility for failure (**situational attribution**)
Just-World Hypothesis	The belief that the world is a fair place and whatever happens to people is what they deserve.
Halo Effect	An evaluator ascribes a positive evaluation to a person based on **dispositional attributes.**
Self-Fulfilling Prophecy	A belief or expectation that helps bring about its reality.
Pygmalion Effect	A type of self-fulfilling prophecy in which expectations of a leader lead to superior performance by their subordinates.

Foot-in-the-Door-Phenomenon	People are more likely to comply with a large request if someone first asks them to comply with a smaller one.
Door-in-the-Face-Phenomenon	People are more likely to comply with a reasonable request if they deny someone an extreme request.

9.2 How are attitudes formed and changed?

Cognitive Dissonance	• **Leon Festinger** • People need to maintain consistency in their cognitive systems. • One needs to alleviate the tension when one's behavior and beliefs are inconsistent.

Central Route to Persuasion	Forming or changing attitudes based on a thoughtful evaluation of their merits
Peripheral Route to Persuasion	Forming or changing attitudes based on cues outside of the merits and without careful scrutinizing of the relevant information

| | Little Elaboration | Extensive Elaboration |

Elaboration Likelihood Model	• Attitude change occurs on a continuum from little scrutiny/**elaboration** to extensive scrutiny/**elaboration**. • Scrutiny/**elaboration** determines peoples' **attitude** strength. • Little Elaboration • Extensive Elaboration
Elaboration	The process of thinking about the merits of relevant information Note- This type of **elaboration** differs from **elaboration** as a cognitive science study technique described in Unit 5.

9.3 How do the situational influences of conformity, compliance, and obedience influence behavior?

Conformity	Changing opinions, judgments, and behavior to become consistent with the others in a group or situation
Norms	The values and unwritten rules of behavior for a group or situation

Asch Situation	• **Solomon Asch** • An experiment in which participants answer questions as part of a group of confederates who deliberately answer incorrectly. Measures the degrees that participants **conform** to the **group norms**. • See below- Confederates would all state that line "A" matched when the participant could see that the answer was "C." Close to 32% conformed to the wrong answer.	(image of Asch line experiment: reference line on left; comparison lines A, B, C on right) Fred the Oyster, Asch experiment, CC BY-SA 4.0

Normative Social Influence	• Internalizing the group **norms,** so one feels compelled to behave, think, and feel in ways that are consistent with the group. • Rejecting the group **norms** often results in ridicule and **ostracism.** • Society rewards those that **conform**.
Informative Social Influence	The process of change in thinking or behavior as a result of persuasion of information
Reciprocity Norm	The expectation is that when people help others, they will receive equal help in return.
Social-Responsibility Norm	The standard set by society is that one should assist those in need even if they may not repay it.
Social Exchange Theory	Social behavior is an exchange in which one maximizes benefits and minimizes costs.

Obedience	Complying with a direct command by a person in a position of authority	
Behavioral Study of Obedience	• **Stanley Milgram** • He assigned participants as teachers who had to deliver an electric shock to examinees for incorrect answers. • Participants did not administer shocks. The confederates made them believe that they were shocking them. • The magnitude of shocks increased with each incorrect answer. • The experimenter said to the participant that they should continue if they appeared to question what they were doing. • 63% delivered the most lethal voltage of 450 volts.	anonymous, Milgram Experiment, CC BY-SA 3.0

Stanford Prison Study	• **Phillip Zimbardo** • Tests the power of the situation to determine behavior. • He **randomly assigned** participants to the **role** of prison guards or prisoners. • The two-week experiment was terminated after six days because the participants showed psychological trauma. | **Prison Guards**	**Prisoners**
---	---
Demeaning language	Docile, subservient
Humiliation techniques	Begged to be paroled
Push-ups as punishments	Uncontrollable crying
Stripped prisoners naked	Staged a revolt and escape plan
Placed prisoners in solitary confinement	They gave up and became hopeless
Woke the prisoners in the middle of the night			Philip Zimbardo, SPE1971-prisoner-4325-in-prison-smock, CC BY-SA 4.0
Role	A set of behaviors expected of an individual based on their position	
Lucifer Effect	The power of social contexts to negatively change behavior	

9.4 How does the presence of others affect individual behavior?

Social Facilitation	- The improvement on a task in the presence of others - Works best when tasks are well-rehearsed or easy.
Social Loafing	The tendency to put forth less effort when working in a group compared to working alone
Deindividuation	A loss of self-awareness and self-restraint that results from anonymity or blending in with a group
Group Polarization	The tendency for people's beliefs to become stronger as they discuss them in a group of like-minded individuals
Group Think	The tendency of groups to maintain harmony and thus, individuals do not present dissenting views. It can lead to poor decision-making.
Bystander Effect	- A tendency of individuals to fail to deliver assistance to those in need when others are present - Emergencies - Confusion or **diffusion of responsibility**
Diffusion of Responsibility	Feeling less accountable for duties when in the presence of others

***Study Tip-* Semantic Encoding/Elaboration**: There are many examples of these phenomena in the news, history, and everyday life. Find one example of each of the terms above to remember them better. Can you think of one example you learned in history class for any of these terms?

Social Traps	Once established, a course of action between individuals, groups, or governments is difficult to stop even though it could lead to lethal consequences.
Game Theory	- A branch of mathematics that analyzes how decision-makers affect each other. - Many applications to various fields, including psychology
Zero-Sum Game	In **game theory,** players' decisions lead to equal gains and losses. For someone to win, someone else has to lose.
Non-Zero-Sum	In **game theory,** when players' decisions do not balance
Prisoner's Dilemma	- Example of **game theory**. - Two suspects are separated. - The one who confesses will receive a heavy sentence, and the other will go free. - If both confess, they will receive a moderate sentence. - If neither confesses, they will escape with a light sentence. Christopher X Jon Jensen (CXJJensen) & Greg Riestenberg, Prisoner's Dilemma embezzlement, CC BY-SA 3.0

Conflict	When the actions or beliefs of individuals are viewed as unacceptable by the other side
Conflict Resolution	Efforts to reduce friction by negotiating, bargaining, and conciliation
Superordinate Goals	Members of two or more groups work together and pool their skills to accomplish a goal they cannot achieve alone.
Graduated and Reciprocated Initiatives in Tension-Reduction (GRIT)	An approach to resolving group conflict that involves: communication between the parties, cooperative intentions, carrying out the intentions, and cooperative responses even during competition.

9.5 What factors contribute to bias, prejudice, and discrimination?

Bias	A feeling for or against something or someone
Stereotype	A set of cognitive beliefs about the qualities and characteristics of a group and its members
Prejudice	Pre-judge. A negative attitude toward another person or group without any experience with them
Discrimination	Treating others differently based on some group characteristic

In-Group/Out-Group Bias	The tendency to favor one's group and view those outside the group as inferior
Ethnocentrism	Viewing one's ethnic, racial, or national group as the center of everything
Scapegoat Theory	The tendency to blame one's negative experiences on other groups
Mere-Exposure Effect	Individuals demonstrate a more favorable attitude toward something or someone with repeated exposure.

9.6 What is altruism?

Altruism	An unselfish behavior that benefits others and costs oneself.

What is aggression, and what contributes to it?

Aggression	<ul><li>Behavior intended to harm others physically or psychologically.</li><li>Causes are varied: **genetics, testosterone**, alcohol, brain injuries such as **CTE**, frustration, aggressive role models, **deindividuation**, minimal father involvement, rejection, temperature, and reinforced behavior.</li></ul>
Frustration-Aggression Hypothesis	<ul><li>Frustration produces an aggressive urge.</li><li>Aggression is always the result of frustration.</li></ul>
Aggression-Frustration Hypothesis	Frustration must be unpleasant to produce aggression.

9.7 What factors contribute to attraction and love?

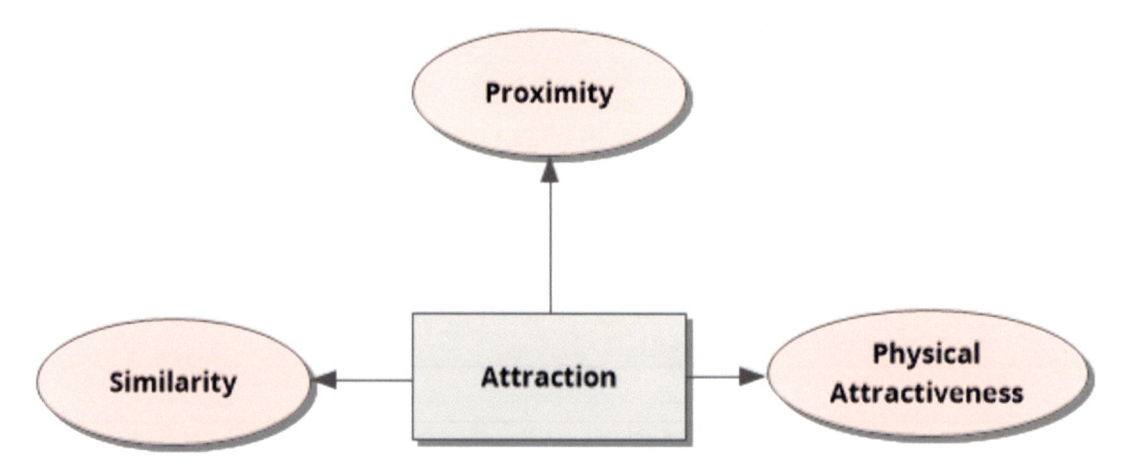

Attraction → Proximity, Similarity, Physical Attractiveness

Passionate Love	<ul><li>Emotional arousal and sexual passion are core features.</li><li>More intense emotions</li><li>**Two-Factor Theory of Emotion**</li></ul>
Companionate Love	Strong feelings of intimacy and affection for another

Equity	A condition when people receive what they give equally.
Self-Disclosure	The process of revealing personal and private information about oneself to others

References

American Psychological Assocation. (2022). *American Psychological Association.* Retrieved from APA Dictionary of Psychology: https://dictionary.apa.org/

Mayo Clinic. (2022). Retrieved from Mayo Clinic: https://www.mayoclinic.org/

Open Stax. (2022, May 5). Retrieved from Open Stax: https://openstax.org/books/psychology/pages/1-2-history-of-psychology

ScienceFacts.Net/Synapse. (2021, June 18). Retrieved from ScienceFacts.net: https://www.sciencefacts.net/wp-content/uploads/2020/05/Synapse-Diagram.jpg

Walinga, J. (2014, October 17). *Open Text BC Campus.* Retrieved from https://opentextbc.ca/introductiontopsychology/chapter/3-1-the-neuron-is-the-building-block-of-the-nervous-system/

Made in the USA
Columbia, SC
16 July 2024